Barriers To Love

A Spiritual View Of Prejudice
With Spiritual Solutions

Cover © 1997 Sandra St. John
Photo © 1993 Glamour Shots
First edition
First printing 1997
Editors: Jill Klunder and Gayle Bachicha

Printed in the United States of America
by McNaughton & Gunn

Tickerwick Publications
P.O. Box 100695
Denver, CO 80250

Library of Congress Cataloging-in-Publication Data

St. John, Sandra
   Barriers to love : a spiritual view of prejudice with spiritual
solutions / Sandra St. John. -- 1st ed.
      p.   cm.
   Includes bibliographical references.
   ISBN 1-885084-44-7 (pbk.)
   1. Sexism--Religious aspects--Controversial literature.
2. Homophobia--Religious aspects--Controversial literature.
3. Spiritual life.   I. Title.
BL65.S4S7   1996
291.1'7834--dc20   96-15635
                                                         CIP

Barriers To Love

A Spiritual View of Prejudice
With Spiritual Solutions

Sandra St. John, Ed.D.

Acknowledgments

I wish to acknowledge and to thank all of my spiritual teachers. Many have graced me with their presence and knowledge through the written word of their books. While it would be too numerous to mention all of them, of special significance is Dr. Emmet Fox. Other contemporary teachers from whom I have had the pleasure of learning through lecture and seminar work are Rev. Edwene Gaines and Dr. Michael Ryce. Their work is truly outstanding.

In spite of the format of male gender bias, the one greatest vehicle for personal healing which I have thus far experienced is the *Course In Miracles*. To do so, I have changed the male references to those devoid of gender. I give special thanks to the Foundation for Inner Peace for making this work available and I encourage them to create a version without gender bias. The message of this work is truly inspiring.

Most importantly, I give thanks to the Mother-Father Source of my being and to my own Inner Teacher, the part of the Source which I AM. Thank you for inspiring me through the many Master Teachers from all religions, the ones who came to serve and to teach the importance of love, forgiveness and the ethical treatment of self and all others through the practice of the Golden Rule. May all of us learn to practice it now without exclusion of anyone. May we always be willing to help each other to love, to forgive and to be of greater service in the world. Blessings!

Sandra St. John

Introduction

     This book is a serious quest for spiritual values amid the many faces of prejudice on planet earth. How and why have we created so many barriers to love? We can view the prejudice in ourselves and/or the world by becoming aware of everything which is considered to be "better than" that: this religion, this gender, this sexual orientation, this race, this color or this person over that one. Why is it that we are so quick to say "better than" instead of "different from", especially when "better than" so often attaches itself to hatred, anger and violence? "Better than" gives birth to judgment, which then precedes prejudicial action. All are born from irrational thought. Why are we so prone to think irrationally?

     We could not have chosen "better than" over "different from" unless we felt separate from each other and we could not have embraced those separating thoughts unless we felt separated from the Source of our being, the Source of all good. As we separated from that goodness, we ceased to do good. When did such a separation begin?

     When we began to envision our masculine and feminine qualities as separate, we created separation in ourselves. We then empowered ourselves to value these male and female qualities differently. Endowing the Source of our being (from whom we had already separated) with our identical and irrational values provided the nurturing soil from which our prejudices could grow. Gender prejudice, or sexism, then became the parent of all forms of prejudice, and was sanctioned by the deity, no less. By separating the masculine and feminine in ourselves, the Source of all good was forgotten and prejudice was born. It is one of the most interesting of paradoxes that the Godly gender creates barriers to love. Historically, the three most prominent barriers have been made from the fabric of education, power and money.

     The most flagrant form of prejudice has always been sexism. From this parental form, all other forms of prejudice evolved or "this became better than that". The most extreme form of all of them is that of homosexual prejudice. In some ways, it is surprising that sexual activities in which heterosexuals involve themselves becomes abhorrent when homosexually practiced. In other ways, it is not so surprising at all. At a profoundly deep level, it speaks of that initial separation of the masculine and feminine principles in ourselves and of our separation from the Source, Itself.

No amount of recognition or understanding can ever serve as validation for any form of prejudice because it does not allow us to treat others as we, ourselves, would be treated. This is the spiritual standard against which we must measure all of our behavior. It is the purpose of *Barriers To Love* to serve as that remembrance and to shed light, that we might choose to create a path of love and respect for everyone on our journey to the *light*.

It is the author's belief that until we are able to contemplate the deity devoid of gender, we cannot eliminate the many forms of prejudice that exist in the world. Sexism is the parent of all prejudice. It is the beginning of "this is better than that". Until we heal this irrational thought, we cannot move forth in our consciousness of love. The parent of prejudice gave birth to many children in the world to which those of different race, color, religion and sexual orientation can attest.

Two specific areas of exploration for *Barriers To Love* are sexism and homosexual prejudice. If we can understand these two prejudicial forms enough to heal our own personal barriers to love, there is no doubt that we can eliminate all forms of prejudice in the world. It is a noble goal of which we are all worthy of arriving. Toward this end, *Barriers To Love* is appropriate reading material for every individual who experiences prejudice for any reason and for everyone who holds prejudice against anyone, any group or anything. This book offers the reader an opportunity to examine the subject from a spiritual perspective and to assess his/her own prejudices. It also presents some tools which may be helpful in achieving wholeness. *Barriers To Love* is offered to the world with love.

Sandra St. John

Dedication

This book is fondly dedicated to all of the Mothers
in the world,

Especially to:

My own mother, Ana

My second mother, Titi Lucy

My departed other mother, Dorothy

and to the

Earth Mother, Herself.

All of you are remembered with love *forever*.

CONTENTS:

CHAPTER ONE

The Nature of Prejudice

Throughout the many centuries of life on earth, there has evolved but one spiritual truth which all civilizations and most human beings have consistently failed to practice. It is a simple and beautiful truth which everyone recognizes as a conscionable way to live, yet we still resist taking it on as the pattern for our life experience. We know this spiritual teaching as the Golden Rule but our feeling about it is too often more reactive than proactive. This has insured its failure in the world. Our motto has become: "I shall begin treating others as they would like to be treated when they start treating me that way". We somehow extrapolate this into poetic license to avoid the practice of ethical and loving behavior toward others and, we might further conclude, this absence of love is the nature of prejudice.

We have bartered the Golden Rule for power over others and for material increase. We have sold it for thirty pieces of silver. We have killed others and waged wars by rationalizing our purpose for doing so. There have been many exceptions cited as valid reasons for not practicing the spiritual truth we have so futilely tried to learn. We have often done so in God's name, as though this somehow made a difference, and we have hoped that no one would notice our ungodly behavior for what it was. We have vigorously defended it whenever we needed to do so.

As a human race, we have failed to treat others as we desire to be treated. We have presented many, many different excuses for not practicing the Golden Rule "in this particular instance". Our separation from the Source of our being has allowed our childishness and indulged us in our arrogance of assumed correctness. This has ensured our failure to live by this noble spiritual standard. We have blamed others for our bad behavior. It has so often been "their fault".

All the while, our souls have cried out through our minds and hearts: "This is important for us to learn". Why can we not learn to treat others as we would be treated? Why do we choose to adulterate the Golden Rule with the lesser metals of the earthly plane? Why do we not keep it golden and pure? This is what is necessary to become a loving human being. Is this not the very thing that we are seeking for ourselves? Is this not representative of our own quest for love? Our error comes in perceiving that love is to be found outside ourselves. It is a common error easily made in a material world.

Endlessly, we seek for love in the world. We look here; we look there. "Where is it, we ask?" We mistake it for sex, power and money. This is ultimately disappointing. After a while, we begin to ask: "Why do others mistreat and abuse me"? "Why", we ask, "are people no damned good?" We go on to draw many conclusions about love which have more to do with fear, as we go on seeking. "Why can we not find love?"

The answer is a simple one. We cannot find love until we are love. We cannot see evidence of it in the world until we experience it in ourselves. We cannot welcome it at our door until we give it. Look into the mirror and what do you see? You see "you", don't you? Life is exactly the same. Look at life now, and what do you see? If you see pain and suffering, maltreatment from others, and people whom are no damned good, guess what? This is how you are reflecting in the world. You are looking at a deep part of yourself just aching to be healed.

We are looking in the mirror, but as long as we do not realize it, we shall see the reflection of what appears as the property of others. No wonder we do not practice the Golden Rule, "they" do not deserve it!

Our souls always know better, even if we do not consciously see the truth. A part of us knows that it is important to treat others as we would be treated. In those moments when we do, we experience peace and joy and most of all, the thing we seek called love. We cannot experience this kind of love in any other way. For instance, when we seek love through power, rather than treating others as we would be treated, we often take unfair advantage and therefore, we create fear. Fear is then what returns to us, not love. There is great truth to the principle that like attracts like in the universe.

There are moments when we give love and love is what we experience. How wonderful it feels, but all too soon it is that we forget how we arrived here. Too soon our wheels go off the track; life becomes the bumpy ride that we remember and people, once again, are no damned good! Somehow, we need to find a way to give extended life to the remembrance of how it felt to give to others from a loving heart.

Where might we look for guidance on this most important Golden Rule, that we might learn to practice it more consistently? How might we learn to change the base metal of our life's experience into pure gold? Religions speak of love and they also speak of the importance of ethical treatment of others. If religions are in agreement that this is a worthy goal, should we not take it even more seriously? Because they speak of its importance, it must be what they do. If we but notice how they have ridden this bicycle, surely, we shall become more capable of riding it. Perhaps this can become our model for adherence to the Golden Rule?

As we begin this quest, we are confronted with many strange inconsistencies. Going back in time as far as we are able to the days of the Goddess religions, we find that women seemed to be the powerful gender in both economic and sexual terms. Only women were allowed to minister to the deity, who was, Herself, a woman. Maybe Goddess worshippers believed in treating others as they would be treated, but it would appear that this practice was not totally extended to the males of their society. Men could not have been happy about this. Somehow, this does not appear to be the place where we can learn the whole truth about the Golden Rule in action.

Perhaps we shall find the truth of practicing the Golden Rule through the God of Abraham? It is very interesting that God is no longer female but the Hebrews are still talking about the value of the Golden Rule. Perhaps they have discovered something unknown to the Goddess worshippers. The Israelites surely are practicing the ethical treatment of others, but how can they be with so much violence, especially against those Goddess worshippers in Canaan? Only the Hebrew men are teachers and interpreters for God and He too is male. It is forbidden to teach women nor are they worthy of direct communication with God, except through men. It seems to be related to some strange story about her being made from his rib. Why, women are even owned by men! Wait a minute. Isn't this slavery? Is this not what they left in Egypt? Why are they doing the same thing to their women? Is this a case of the abused becoming the abuser? Could this be related to some kind of retaliation against the Goddess worshippers? Oh my God, they even thank God in their daily prayers for not making them slaves, gentiles or women. This sounds like sexism and racism. What about the Levite priests? They seemed to have such a hatred of homosexuals! As a matter of fact, they sound very controlling of all areas of life, and the penalty for almost everything is death! All of this does not seem very representative of the Golden Rule. This may be the original inception of a forked tongue.

The Hebrews did consider the Golden Rule and the ethical treatment of others to be important. They simply excluded from its practice slaves, gentiles, women and homosexuals. Their attempts to treat others as they would be treated seemed to be intended only for other Jewish men who also practiced the Jewish religion as well as the same prejudices. This does not seem to be a good model for the practice of the Golden Rule for there are too many exclusions. Not only is an entire gender excluded, as was the case with Goddess worshippers (we can understand that the gender exclusion would flip-flop), in addition to sexism, there is racism and classism. Could it be that one form of prejudice seems to give rise to another?

As we continue our quest through time and religions, we shall continue to seek a model with no exclusions to the practice of the Golden Rule. The message of Jesus Christ sounds perfect. He seems to have really understood our need to live by the Golden Rule, even though God was still exclusively male, or so we have been told through our holy books. I bet He would have rectified this situation had he not died so young. Why did the Jews kill him when he was also a Jew? I guess that they killed him because he pointed out their non-compliance of the Golden Rule and because his opinion of God was different from theirs. That God was love and not fear seems to have been both innovating and blasphemous.

As we look to the early Christian church which was formed to carry forth the message of Jesus, and later, to the Catholic Church, we find an even more entrenched and protracted exclusion of women in their practice of the Golden Rule as well as intolerance of other religious faiths through the cruelty and violence of the Crusades. It is unbelievable that they were perpetrated in the name of God. Was this a problem of too much testosterone gone berserk? We still have sexism, classism, racism and name-calling of other religions. The Muslims were called infidels or those having no religious beliefs. Does this not sound like gross intolerance of beliefs unlike their own? This does not seem like an excellent format for the practice of the Golden Rule. How did Christians manage to lose the message of Jesus Christ? How did the message manage to lose the messenger?

The Christians would enter their own internal power struggle against the authority of the papacy. The two most powerful bones of contention were man's ability to commune directly with God without the Catholic priest being a mandatory agent in this process and the Catholic's sale of power and influence peddling under the guise of pilgrimages. A full scale revolt known as the Reformation would begin in the 1500s when the German monk, Martin Luther, attacked the Pope's authority and asserted that each believer could commune directly with God. What a novel idea and what a commotion this caused! While this gave rise to the Lutheran Church which lanced some of the boils of prejudice and unrighteous behavior, it did not take care of the entire problem. We cannot forget that it was the ideas of Martin Luther which fueled anti-Semitism in Germany and elsewhere. Such was clearly an aberration and an abandonment of the Golden Rule entirely. We have the continuation of sexism, classism and even the more horrific manifestations of racism in practice. It is extremely interesting that the most important American black leader of the 20th Century, whom would lead a non-violent confrontation against racism, would have the name of Martin Luther. The triumphant symbolism evoked by the contemplation of this event gives hope to humanity that the Golden Rule is still the standard of excellence for which to strive.

John Calvin effected his own revolt from which came the Presbyterians. The Church of England broke with the Pope on the issue of power and from this break was formed the Anglican Church, whose American version became the Episcopalians. John Bunyan broke with the Anglican Church to give rise to the Baptist faith. George Fox established the Society of Friends. They would become known as the Quakers, from which the American Congregationalists, Unitarians and Universalists came. The last large faith to emerge from the revolution were the Methodists under John Wesley.

It could be said that these religious and historical events come into being because of non-compliance and non-practice of the Golden Rule. It should strengthen our faith that humankind shall never abandon this quest. It continues to be the basis on which religions are formed, reformed and the reason why some simply pass away. Then and now, there remains much work to be done.

The Catholics were shocked by the audacity of all of those whom dared to disagree. They began a period of reform while they also attacked the growth of Protestantism. This would become known as the Counter Reformation. It included the development of an offensive position through the establishment of missionaries to advance church membership. In the 20th Century, this could be contemplated as the foundation for marketing techniques in the business world and lobbyists in the political arena. In the last two decades of the 20th Century in the United States of America, the religious right would attempt a fusion of these processes to advance their religious agenda. The concept of "separation of church and state" would again become a bulls-eye for target practice. Would it fail as it had so many times in the past? Would Americans forget the violent and costly lessons of their ancestors? This drama continues to unfold as we approach the New Millennium.

There would be many wars fought between the Catholics and the Protestants which still, to this day, continue. Let us also not forget the many Fundamentalists of all faiths (often called Republicans in America), whom surpass all religions in their perpetration of sexism and racism claims in the world. It is particularly noticeable in the fight against a woman's right to make choices regarding her body.

Clear contemporary examples are to be found in the fight over abortion, the reluctance to allow laws to protect homosexuals, the insensitivity to the plight of the poor and disenfranchised and the willingness to allow any form of racism, classism and sexism to continue. Many are still "more equal than others". They are still male, white, heterosexual and affluent and they advance political agendas which preserve their own characteristics. Many of their exponents are from the Religious Right and espouse an ideology which must be rejected by women whom would be free. They inject God into their prejudicial process to justify their material thoughts and actions. Some have even killed in the name of God. This is truly a mixing of metaphors unworthy of the deity. Prejudice can never serve as a vehicle for the ethical treatment of others.

Is there nowhere to be found an exemplary model of the practice of the Golden Rule among the many messengers for God? There is one simple spiritual truth of great importance and even the religions of the world (and many politicians) do not seem to be able to practice it. Are we to conclude that religions, as well as people are no damned good? Are they much different from Genghis Khan, who believed himself to be a descendent from God and did terrible things, in his name or Attila the Hun, whom upon finding what he believed to be the Sword of God, interpreted this as his destiny to conquer the world? Is "God" how man justifies his bad behavior?

Religions have given us the idea that the Golden Rule is important and this standard has become a compatible component in all the great religions of the world. Human beings, of all faiths, also recognize the importance of this teaching. The personal problem in this, for many, is that there is so much evidence that religions, faiths and churches have not practiced what they have preached and we have modeled our behavior in this light.

Why is this so? What, we might ask, stands in the way of practicing the Golden Rule? What stands in our consciousness as a barrier to love for all people at all times? The answer can be found in one word: *prejudice*. It gives rise to barriers to love through its distorted view of life. It causes us to separate from the Source of our being whom would not condone, for any reason, the exclusion of ethical treatment of anyone or any group.

What exactly is prejudice and what is its nature? *The New College Edition of The American Heritage Dictionary* defines it as follows: "1. a. An adverse judgment or opinion formed beforehand or without knowledge or examination of the facts. b. A preconceived preference or idea; bias. 2. The act or state of holding unreasonable preconceived judgments or convictions. 3. Irrational suspicion or hatred of a particular group, race or religion. . .(as a verb) 1. To cause (someone) to judge prematurely and irrationally; to bias. 2. To affect injuriously or detrimentally by some judgment or act."

We find that prejudice is derived from the word judgment or "to judge". Prejudicial judgment is emotionally derived from fear. In this context, both fear and judgment are irrational. Prejudice can then be understood through a four step process. It begins with an irrational thought which then engenders fear amplified by emotion. This leads to judgment based upon those fears from which is evoked prejudicial action. Here is a visual model of how it operates in the world.

PREJUDICE:

> **1. Irrational Thought(s)**
>
> **2. Fear(s)+ Emotion(s)**
>
> **3. Judgment(s)**
>
> **4. Prejudicial Action(s)**

We cannot have prejudice without first having an irrational thought. If we again look in *The American Heritage Dictionary*, we find irrational defined as: "1. a. Not endowed with reason. b. Affected by loss of usual or normal mental clarity; incoherent, as from shock. c. Contrary to reason; illogical: *an irrational dislike.* 2. a. Designating a syllable in Greek and Latin prosody whose length does not fit the metrical pattern..."

From these definitions, we can see that an irrational thought need have no basis in reality. For instance, a mentally unstable individual may see bugs crawling all over the wall which are not, in reality, there. This is an irrational thought. Once the individual experiences the irrational thought and accepts it as reality, he/she can then go on to experience fear. "They are going to harm me!" It is after the individual has experienced some form of fear, and has combined it with emotion, that he/she can then experience judgment: "These bugs are bad things!" Judgment usually assumes the form of "good" or "bad" and, in this context, it leads to prejudicial action. The individual, with shoe in hand, may then attempt to kill all of the bugs on the wall. Judgment has often taken the form of "death".

The above is an analytical example of how prejudice works. Beginning with a thought which has no basis in reality, we then become fearful of it, combine it with emotion, make judgments about it and then, we take action upon these judgments. We might question, "Could this procedure ever assist us in arriving at the truth when we begin from an irrational assumption"? The author thinks not and yet, such a model is used and abused on every group and everything against which we hold prejudice.

For instance, let us briefly look at racial prejudice in the form of anti-Semitism. The irrational thought (at least for some Christians) might be: "They crucified Jesus." This is an irrational thought because all Jews certainly did not crucify Jesus. To hold responsible the entire Jewish race because some Jews crucified Jesus cannot, by any standard, be considered rational or ethical. If one accepts the irrational thought as reality, however, one can then begin to fear the Jewish race, accompany this with great emotion and make judgments about Jews. "They are not good people!" Once the judgment is made, the ones judging are free to persecute them through prejudicial actions. History tells us that such activity has happened over and over again and has often led to death.

Does such prejudice make sense? Is killing innocent people ever justified? Is killing, for any reason, ever justified? The act can only be as rational as the thought which created it. Anti-Semitism, as well as every other form of prejudice, begins from an irrational idea which we allow to trick us into believing it is so. Prejudice, therefore, can never make sense because its parent is nonsensical. Its genetic composition is seriously flawed.

If ever there was a generation any more inclined to dispose of irrational ideas which do not make logical sense, our scientific and high-tech culture should be well equipped to do so. There is no logic to be found in doing otherwise. The fact that it has not yet been done speaks to the matter that this is not solely an issue of the mind, but also one of the heart. There is emotion attached to the irrational thought(s). All of us are in touch with how emotion can cloud the issue from which judgment springs. We might further conclude that if our emotions and judgments cause us to treat anyone in ways that we would not wish to be treated, such emotions are, indeed, in need of healing.

Homosexual prejudice might be described as the most emotionally charged and the most extreme form of prejudice which exists in our society. Using the four step model, an example of this might be viewed as follows:

PREJUDICE (Homosexual)

1. **Irrational Thoughts**: They will not reproduce
   through their sexual expression and the human race
   will become extinct. They are sexually promiscuous
   and my minister/rabbi says God does not approve of
   them.

2. **Fear**: They may be sexually interested in me or

in my children. *Charge with emotion*.

> **3. Judgment**: Homosexuals are depraved
> and "bad" persons. God hates them and so do I.

> **4. Prejudiced Actions**: I shall physically "gay
> bash" every chance I get and I shall speak
> out against them. They do not belong in the
> military and they should not be
> protected under the law in the same
> way that I am. They should stay
> "in the closet", etc.

Notice some of the feelings, beliefs and actions which stem from irrational thoughts and begin to analyze them. The fact that homosexual behavior will not lead to procreation is not a rational thought on which to base hate. Not all homosexuals are sexually promiscuous. This thought also is irrational when one applies it to the whole population of homosexual persons. Because one's minister/rabbi, or anyone in authority, voices God's disapproval of homosexuals does not make this a rational thought. How can anyone speak for God in an unloving manner? Is this not more a matter of man's ideas being attributed to God?

The deity has inspired all religions to treat others as they would be treated. Is this such an example? Any intelligent and loving person will quickly see that every form of prejudice goes against this spiritual truth. It is precisely prejudice which creates our barriers to love. Prejudicial behavior is contradictory in spiritual terms to what it means to be a loving human being. Chapter 2 will deal, more specifically, with the basis for homosexual prejudice through an exploration of our spiritual heritage.

Before continuing on to the second chapter, the reader is encouraged to explore his/her prejudices against women, homosexuals, blacks, disabled individuals and any other individual, group or thing from the perspective of the four step model. The purpose for doing so is one of self revelation. It is not easy to dispel our prejudices if we distance ourselves from our irrational thoughts and fail to see them for what they are. We must accept that they are at work in our interior landscape if we are able to hold prejudice against any individual, group or thing. Getting in touch with our irrational thoughts is the beginning of the end of prejudice on earth.

For example, think of something or someone about whom you know you harbor prejudice and fill in the blanks for yourself.

PREJUDICE:

1. Irrational Thought(s)

2. Fear(s) + Emotion(s)

3. Judgment(s)

4. Prejudicial Action(s)

As we move the focus of our minds from our prejudicial feelings, beliefs and actions to the irrational thought(s) which created our prejudice(s), we can find our way back to love and fair treatment of all others. Our soul truly longs for this. Without even planning to do so, we shall find ourselves more capable of practicing the Golden Rule more easily and effortlessly. Joyously, we shall find ourselves riding this bicycle with no hands!

Prejudice is that insidiously hateful thing which enables us to create barriers to the expression of love for everyone. While there are many different reasons why one would desire to express love to everyone, the reason we can all agree upon is that love feels better than fear. It is important that we eliminate prejudice from our lives so that we can become all that we can be: love, and the Golden Rule in action. This begins with self love which then allows us to love others as we dispel the illusions of the world. Life then becomes a grand opportunity to return to more of what we really are. Becoming love in action creates a different life.

While there are many forms of prejudice in the world, it is not the intent of this book to examine all of them in detail. The model for addressing them, however, remains the same. Where there is prejudice, there is irrational thought. As we own this idea and address the irrational thought within us, we are able to eliminate prejudice within ourselves and in the world.

It is the purpose of this book to examine both the oldest form of prejudice and the most extreme and emotionally charged prejudicial form. It is the author's intent to examine prejudice against women and against homosexuals from a spiritual perspective. Gender prejudice is the oldest form of irrational thought and it contributes to the distancing of men and women. Since the beginning of the God of Abraham, women have been the prejudiced gender. Homosexual prejudice is perhaps the most extreme form of irrational thought which contributes to the spiritual malpractice of everyone whom fails to apply the Golden Rule to their treatment of this group.

The basis for irrational thought in both forms of prejudice finds its beginnings in the past. We find evidence of this within our holy books. Upon this foundation rest our barriers to love. This does not make them irrelevant or invaluable. They are our spiritual heritage but do we really believe there is prejudice in God? This would certainly be incompatible with the very essence of the Golden Rule. *Barriers To Love* is about addressing differences and inconsistencies in our beliefs and our behavior, so that we might again consciously return to our natural state of perfect love.

This text is not intended to be a definitive, historical document but rather a stroll through the past that we might better understand the present, hopefully, to arrive at a point of view where personal healing becomes possible. In our hearts we know that there is no justifiable reason for prejudice of any kind; however, the responsibility to heal our prejudices is very much a matter of personal choice. We shall not heal them unless we desire to do so; however, if we accept the challenge, this is how we shall unlock the door to the expanded realization of our true nature. When our thoughts are no longer irrational, there will be no more prejudice in our world. Once we address some irrationalities of our spiritual past, we may feel ready to address some ideas for regaining wholeness and strengthening our faith in the Source of our being and in ourselves.

The spiritual ideas presented later in this book are non-denominational in nature and are intended to be supportive of the individual in his/her quest for truth regardless of the religious faith embraced. It is the author's desire to strengthen the relationship between the individual and his/her deity through a thoughtful and an intentional elimination of personal prejudice.

Before continuing to Chapter 2, it is recommended that you work individually with your ownership of prejudice through the four step model for as long as ideas come to mind. When they cease to surface or if you are not consciously led to what your prejudices are, you might ask yourself some of the following questions and let your answers lead you through the four step process.

1. Are there individuals or groups of individuals of whom I am afraid?

2. Whom do I put down through the use of humor?

3. Whom would be my least desirable neighbors?

4. Are there any particular groups of people of whom I do not approve? Identify.

5. Do I believe that any race is superior or inferior
   to any other race? Identify.

6. When I go out in public, would I choose not to sit
   next to a disabled person? Why?

7. Are some types of work unsuitable for a
   particular gender? Identify.

8. Do I treat my son differently than I treat my daughter?

9. Is there any good excuse for anyone not finding a job?

10. Is there anyone I would intentionally harass?

11. Do I believe that laws should be passed which limit a
    man's ability to make decisions about his body?

12. Am I against abortion because I am certain I know
    the exact moment the soul enters the body? On
    whose authority does my knowledge rest?

13. Do I believe that rape is a spiritual practice condoned
    by God?

14. Do I believe that gays and lesbians should stay
    "in the closet"? Why?

15. Is my God masculine or feminine? Why?

This is not meant to be an exhaustive list but only a stimulus to help you get in touch with some of your prejudices in the event you believe that you do not have any or that you have totally handled the problem. All of us have prejudices because we have learned them from others. There is no castigation which goes along with owning that we have them. Keeping them, however, is quite another matter!

It is important for us to recognize that our prejudices say more about "us" than they do about "them". The filters through which we experience the world are upon our own eyes, minds and hearts. This is evidenced by the divergence of opinion on prejudicial issues. It would be more helpful for each one of us to realize that prejudice is but a lack of love within ourselves. We must become responsible enough to correct the error.

It is time to reconcile our differences and to realize there is no spiritually correct position which would cause us to withhold love from anyone or any group for any reason whatsoever. The standard for correction of all error is: "Do I treat EVERYONE as I would like to be treated?" Claiming this spiritual gold as our own will transmute the base metals of our life experience into something much higher. It shall heal the past, create a different "now" and allow us to move forward into the New Millennium with peace, love and forgiveness. It is the world of our soul's desire.

REFLECTIONS

Mother-Father Source of my being, help me as I now look deeply into the heart of my prejudices so that I might find a better way to live. Help me to melt them down through understanding and to use the created liquid to form a new beginning. Help it to lead me back to what I really am and to all that I can be. Help me to find my natural state of perfect love again and to live from that perspective in the world.

As I love myself, I shall love others. As I respect myself, so shall I respect others. I shall seek more understanding of those different from myself. When I speak to them, I shall look directly into their eyes and I shall connect with a loving soul, just like mine. "The Source in you is the Source in me and we are One." My family is of all colors and all faiths. It is both male and female. It is homo-and heterosexual. It is composed of both perfect and imperfect minds and bodies. My family is the family of humanity and it is good.

If my life is worth expressing, it is worth doing so while holding fast to the highest spiritual law of doing unto others as I would have them do unto me. Help me to always remember that love's extension in the world depends upon my actions in it.

CHAPTER TWO

It Is Written . . .

Why are we here on earth and just what are we supposed to be doing here? What are we to learn from this life experience? Could it possibly be that the purpose of life on earth is to willingly and consistently choose to allow ourselves to feel and to express only love? Could it be that we are here to remove our barriers to love? The history of humankind certainly tells us that there have been many times when we have failed to do so; but if we reflect for a moment upon what truly makes us feel good, we know that feeling and expressing love always seems to facilitate the process and the end result of feeling good. We simply cannot express a kindness toward others without feeling good ourselves. We cannot do a good deed without feeling good about it. We cannot give without receiving. Becoming a conscious expressor of love creates peace, joy and harmony in our world. Why then, do we not always express love?

If we focus upon what does not feel good, we are able to better understand our barriers to love, those areas where expressing love seems especially difficult for us. Such barriers never feel good; they usually cause anger and pain within us. They propel us into judgment and prejudicial actions, as we have seen in Chapter 1, and they have the effect of separating us from others. Whenever we choose to separate or create distance between ourselves and others, we deny ourselves the expression of love.

All of us have such barriers, areas which relate to certain individuals, groups or situations where we feel unwilling or unable to respond with love, compassion and acceptance. Just as our automobile has certain areas where vision is unclear, we also have blind spots in our vision of life. Most of the time, we do not know exactly why. It is not uncommon for us to believe that it just happens to be the way we see life; however it is precisely these blind spots which become our barriers to love. We cannot move past this position until we allow love's light to illuminate the darkness of our vision.

It is interesting to note that at the same time we accept these barriers, we know, at least intellectually, that when we allow ourselves to feel and be loving toward others, it feels good. An example of this would be planning a surprise birthday party for someone special. Such a joyous event allows us to extend ourselves in love. We get caught up in the excitement of pleasing another and this feels wonderful. We also know that when we withhold love from others through our thoughts, feelings and actions, this does not feel good.

An example of this would be gossiping about a co-worker. In doing so, we allow ourselves to settle for less than love's expression. If we did not feel separated from this person, we could not allow this feeling and/or action to express through us. We are over here and they are over there. We are this way; they are that way. It is only out of separation that prejudice can be born.

What we surely know from our experience is that when we give out love, the feeling is joyous and expanding. When we fail to give out love, it becomes reductive and diminishing. Such feelings may be angry, critical and/or depressing. When we express love, it creates more space within us to be loving. When we withhold love, it decreases our ability to respond in a loving manner. Knowing this, why would we choose to restrict ourselves from feeling good? Why do we not always feel able to respond lovingly in all situations and to all individuals? What exactly is it that creates our barriers to love?

The answer is found in our judgments. If they separate us from others, they are based upon irrational thoughts, for love is what we are. The things about which we hold negative judgments cause us to withhold love. The more judgmental we become, the greater are our barriers to love. When the barriers become greater than the amount of love we allow ourselves to express, we often experience anger and/or depression.

One might say that an angry or depressed person has simply allowed him/herself to feel and/or express more judgment than love in relation to self and/or others. One might also conclude that an intensely angry or severely depressed individual may have many irrational thoughts which need healing. Anger and depression are then, the negative end of the "feel good" love continuum. To live at this end of the continuum is our choice. Anger and/or depression are often the experiences of feeling a lack of self love and judgment is the piggy-back on which they ride. If love of self is not present, loving another is too painful. Judgment, we think, helps us to avoid pain. Unfortunately, judgment is the very thing which allows prejudice to continue diminishing us, thus making love even more difficult for us to experience.

We are always in control of the situation but we seldom realize it. How we feel and how much we enjoy life is always related to the tools we are using. We have a choice. We can use either love or judgment as tools for creating the experience of life. Choosing wisely, we can create a masterpiece that looks and feels good. Expressing our humanity through the expression of love creates more love energy within us which seeks greater expression. Expressing through judgment decreases our love energy as it builds itself. One judgment seems to beget another as it voraciously devours our love energy.

As we move through life continuing to decrease our expression of love energy, we prematurely age, become angry, depressed, unhappy people and eventually, we die. Judgment then creates stress and love creates peace. Stress shortens life and love extends life. The same principles are operative in business, politics and religions. We cannot withhold love without diminishing ourselves and the organization that we represent. It may not seem so in the short term, but in the long term, the revelation of this truth prevails. A win-win philosophy is but an example of love creating love.

As we ponder the meaning of life, we are able to evolve a spiritual answer to the question of why we are here. Perhaps the purpose of life is simply to increase our love energy, realizing our connectedness with each other and our oneness with all that is. This is how we shall embrace our "forever" life forever growing in the vitality of what we are. Love is what we are and love is what *is written* upon our hearts. Becoming a full expression of it demands we slay the beastly dragons of judgment and prejudice within us, for they hold at bay the actualization of the beauty that we are. How did these judgments and prejudices enter our lives in the first place? Why have we chosen not to feel good? Why have we claimed anger, depression and pain?

Our judgments begin with the past, with our ancestors for four generations we are told. They are passed on to us biologically through our parents and emotionally through their example (which is far more powerful than what they endeavor to teach us through verbal or written language). Our judgments are also acquired through our environment. Most children give expression to their loving nature quite naturally. Judgment is something children learn from the biases of their parents and their environments.

Children are not born disliking those unlike themselves. Children are not born hating homosexuals, blacks, women, fat persons, poor people or those whom are mentally or physically disadvantaged. These are judgments children learn or acquire through their interaction with their parents, other role models and/or their environment. If children experienced only love from their parents and the world, this is what they would tend to continue to express, for they would not have a frame of reference for its antithesis.

Because we, as adults, hold judgmental attitudes and prejudices against others and these are beliefs which we have learned from others, we can unlearn them and acquire new attitudes and beliefs which are supportive of what *is really written* upon our hearts, the directive to only love. This is the lesson all master teachers came to impart. Expressing only love is experienced in the world as the ethical treatment of all others, the call to action so aptly stated through the Golden Rule.

To be able to live from the perspective of "doing unto others as we would have them do unto us" implies that we "must become like little children", recapturing our natural state of love as we overcome our worldly tendency to judge and prejudice others. It is our responsibility and our heart's desire to undo the erroneous lessons in judgment and prejudice which we have learned. Could this be what Jesus meant when he said that he "had overcome the world"? Could this be how we also are to overcome the world?

While there are many groups of individuals judgmentally prejudiced by society, there is no group more ostracized and hated than homosexuals. They have endured verbal abuse, physical abuse and even death for the manner in which God created them, to such a degree, that many of them live looking out at the expansiveness of the world through the tiny window of their "closet".

Homosexuality is indeed humankind's greatest challenge in overcoming judgment and prejudice in the world. If ever there existed non-practice of the Golden Rule, this group has experienced it. Not only has judgmental prejudice been taught overtly and covertly for centuries but, since the beginning of the patriarchal and monotheistic religions, such prejudice and judgment has been directly attributed to God. Such a paradox deserves exploration if we are indeed to "overcome the world".

If we would juxtapose what *is written on our hearts*, the regenerating power of love, against what *man has written* through his holy books, it shall become apparent that judgment and prejudice are inappropriate to a loving heart and they are certainly inappropriate to a loving God. To this end we shall explore the most commonly quoted biblical references which are often interpreted as God's beliefs regarding homosexuality. We shall explore them as objectively as possible with the desire to shed new light upon these references for the general population, for homosexuals, for religious leaders and anyone whom has interest in broadening their understanding and their capacity to love. In doing so, judgment and prejudice shall be addressed and, hopefully, transmuted into something higher by all parties.

To sit in judgment against others is not something that religions profess to condone and yet, in practice, many of their leaders and proponents do sit in the judgment seat with regard to homosexuality. In doing so, they withhold love and adversely influence others to do so. This is somewhat confusing because of the apparent paradox it creates. Some religious leaders may say that it is not the individual they condemn, but rather, the behavior; however, the individual and the behavior cannot really be separated. Together, they form a sexual orientation; however, it must be stated that there are both, ethical and unethical uses of all orientations. Unethical applications of homosexual or heterosexual activity should not be condoned by anyone.

Why do we not simply condemn all behaviors which are unethical in their treatment of others or which do not adhere to the Golden Rule? Some reasons for this have to do with our unwillingness to think and to investigate for ourselves. It is often easier to be told what to think rather than to independently arrive at alternate conclusions. After all, our conditioning has become a powerful influence in our lives. Other more important reasons having to do with judgment against homosexuality are often touted as being rooted in the holy books, especially those of the Jewish and Christian religions which we call the Bible, but are they really as they have been represented? We shall explore the most quoted of them as they relate to the basis for judgment against homosexuality.

In the first century, Rabbi Hillel succinctly said that the essence of the Torah is: "Do not do unto others what you would not have them do unto you." This is recounted in Karen Armstrong's *A History of God*, an excellent source for the reader. Through the Gospels, we also know that Jesus advocated the Golden Rule of doing unto others as you would have them do unto you. Without a code of conduct which inspires right treatment of others, do we really have any worthwhile religious values? The Golden Rule is such a standard and it is compatible and acceptable to all of the major religions. How well we practice it in relation to our homosexual brothers and sisters often shows the room there is for growth. There are, after all, no exclusions intended in the practice of the Golden Rule.

It is extremely confusing to both Jewish and Christian homosexuals that many proponents of their faith do not practice this essential message of their religious beliefs when it comes to their homosexual members. The essence of their beliefs is clearly put forth in both versions of the Golden Rule. It is the purpose of this chapter to explore some of the reasons why this may be so. In pursuing the written word of the holy books, we shall seek more understanding regarding the reasons why mankind has employed exclusionary poetic license for the interpretation of God's word in relation to homosexuals.

For a large portion of the world's population, homophobia (fear of homosexuals) and current prejudice against homosexuality has, at its core, a literal interpretation of the Bible as viewed through irrational filters. This allows the individual whom holds prejudice to use the Bible in support of those individual prejudices. It seems reasonable to conclude that the prejudice is within man, not God.

While it is the Hebrew belief that the first five books of the Old Testament, known as the Torah, are divine revelation from God through Moses, it is also readily accepted that the Bible was written by man, divinely inspired perhaps and, most certainly, divinely debated by rabbis, priests and clergy throughout history. Throughout these many debates, it has been revised many times to finally arrive in its many present forms and through the many filters on the hearts and minds of the men involved in such revision. While there are different versions of holy books accepted by the various faiths and denominations thereof, all of them create difficulty in adherence to a literal translation because of man's involvement and the many changes which have ensued at his directive. To come to a greater understanding, we shall attempt to explore a literal translation while offering what seem to be appropriate insights.

There are three references in the Old Testament and three references in the New Testament which are the most quoted against homosexuality. The nature of some individuals as homosexual, however, seems to have always existed as part of God's creation. At the same time, prejudice against this group has also stood as a stumbling block to mankind in their practice of the Golden Rule.

We find that the story of destruction of the cities of Sodom and Gomorrah in Genesis is the most misquoted reference on homosexuality and that Leviticus 18: 22 is the most quoted and considered to be the primary reference source in the Old Testament which is believed to express God's disdain for homosexuality. The 20th Chapter of Leviticus deals with punishment for sins. We shall explore all of these sources and contemplate them with regard to the ethical treatment of others.

The New Testament is the primary influence of the Christian faith which is composed of the Roman Catholic, Eastern Orthodox and Protestant religions. While there are many differences in theology among the various Christian denominations, they join in agreement that their faith takes root in the first four books of the New Testament known as the Gospels, the books of Matthew, Mark, Luke and John, and more specifically, the first three which are known as the synoptic gospels. There is no theology to be found in the Gospels. Herein lies the essence of the Christian faith as the life, teaching, death and resurrection of Jesus are reviewed by his disciples, two of whom are believed to be among the original twelve chosen by Jesus, Matthew and John. Mark and Luke did not know Jesus while he walked the earth, but followed afterward and were closely aligned with Paul in the formation of the early Christian church. It is widely believed that Mark was the first gospel to be written. This assumes, of course, that authorship is correctly assigned.

Christians are also in agreement on the importance of the new dispensation brought about by the life and death of the Messiah and Son of God, Jesus Christ. It is predominantly the basis on which Christianity and Judaism disagree. Christianity believes that Jesus was the predicted Messiah who came and will come again, and Judaism is still waiting for the Messiah to come. After the Gospels in the New Testament, more specifically in those books written by Paul, we find the basis for the created dogma and doctrine of the church. The interpretation and implementation thereof is what separates the various denominations of the Christian faith.

There are no references to homosexuality in the Gospels. Jesus had nothing to say on the subject although he did have a great deal to say about judgment. There are, however, three references most quoted in the New Testament as denouncing homosexual behavior. They are Romans 1: 26-27, Corinthians 6: 9-11 and I Timothy 1: 10. It is interesting to note that all three books were written by the same person, the Apostle Paul. He was not one of the original twelve who walked with Jesus. In fact, Paul (originally a Pharisee named Saul) fiercely persecuted Christians until his conversion on the road to Damascus as stated in the book of Acts. Thereafter, he became the apostle most responsible for the establishment of the early church, the one responsible for taking the message of Jesus Christ to the gentiles and the one who created the religion we refer to as Christianity.

There was much controversy surrounding Paul and some disagreement among some of the original disciples. We also find in Paul, the most prolific of authors in the New Testament, having written thirteen of its twenty seven books. The Christian churches, as we know them today, have as much to do with Paul's beliefs as they do with the teachings of Jesus. It can be said that Paul's writings evolved into an elaboration of form for expression of the content, that being, the message of Jesus Christ as perceived by Paul's interpretation of the Gospels. He also added to the content through his interpretations. Under Paul, we have the church becoming a metaphor for his idea of Christ. That Jesus was God in human form was not formally accepted by the church until the fourth century. While the church proclaimed him the Son of God, Jesus chose to refer to himself as the Son of Man.

The Gospels, especially the first three, which relate the story of the life, message, death and resurrection of Jesus Christ can be considered as the most authoritative source of the Christian message and perhaps, even more specifically, the book of Matthew, since its author was believed to be one of the original disciples. It is interesting to note that at this very core of Christianity, there are no references to homosexuality. In condemning homosexuality, Christians make their interpretations of Paul's beliefs more important than those of Jesus.

Our examination of the Old Testament shall begin with Genesis and the story of the corrupt cities of Sodom and Gomorra. Their destruction is alluded to most often by fire and brimstone preachers as God's punishment for homosexuality yet biblical scholars do not support such a thesis. It is rather a condemnation of sexual abuse and sexuality used as a vehicle for worship as was found in the Goddess religions. It also has something to do with treating others inhospitably. One might say that it was gross non-compliance of the Golden Rule or the treating of others as one would not wish to be treated.

We have God sending the angels to Sodom to see if they can find ten righteous men. If not, the city is to be destroyed. We have Lot insisting upon being hospitable to them by taking them into his house and treating them as he would wish to be treated if he were in a city away from home. We have men from the city coming to Lot's door and asking that the men be brought out to them "that we may know them". Lot offers his virgin daughters instead. The door is closed and the angels strike the men blind. The city is ultimately destroyed. If this story yields a condemnation of anything sexual, it should be a condemnation of gang rape and a gross violation of the Golden Rule.

It should be stated that in early rabbinical writings, there is no condemnation of homosexuality with reference to the story of the destruction of Sodom and Gomorra. There is condemnation of the use of sexuality in the worship of God, as was practiced by the High Priestesses of the Goddess religion (often referred to as the temple prostitutes) and there always was condemnation of unethical treatment of others. Rape and inhospitality were two such examples of abuse of the Golden Rule at work in Genesis 19:5. The reader should take it upon him/herself to read these passages beginning with the 18th Chapter of Genesis so that he/she may also take note of Abraham's hospitality to the Lord. If the reader juxtaposes it against the recounted experience of the Lord's messengers in the city of Sodom, he/she may better understand the reason for the destruction of the cities of Sodom and Gomorra as gross neglect of the Golden Rule. Ezekiel 16: 48-50 seems to support this. In speaking of the city of Jerusalem:

> As I live, saith the Lord God, Sodom thy sister hath
> not done, she nor her daughters, as thou hast done,
> thou and thy daughters.
> Behold, this was the iniquity of thy sister Sodom,
> pride, fullness of bread, and abundance of idleness was
> in her and in her daughters, neither did she strengthen
> the hand of the poor and needy.
> And they were haughty, and committed abomination
> before me: therefore I took them away as I saw good.

We continue our examination of the Biblical references to homosexuality with the book of Leviticus, the third book of the Old Testament of the Bible which comes after Exodus, both a part of the Torah, the authoritative holy book for the Jewish religion.

As background for Leviticus, we find in Exodus that the Israelites escaped from Egypt through the Red Sea, traveled through the wilderness and arrived at Mount Sinai where Moses received the ten commandments. From Exodus 20: 3-17, they are as follows:

1. Thou shalt have no other gods before me.

2. Thou shalt not make unto thee any graven image...

3. Thou shalt not take the name of the Lord, thy God, in vain...

4. Remember the sabbath day, to keep it holy.

5. Honour thy father and thy mother.

6. Thou shalt not kill.

7. Thou shalt not commit adultery.

8. Thou shalt not steal.

9. Thou shalt not bear false witness against thy neighbor.

10. Thou shalt not covet thy neighbor's house, wife, manservant, maidservant, nor his ox, ass, nor anything that is thy neighbor's.

Note that the "Thou shalt nots..." do not indicate any circumstances where there are exceptions to be made. The basic teaching of the ten commandments is that there is only one (male) God to be praised and the Golden Rule is the only acceptable code of conduct.

Leviticus, also written by Moses, was given as a handbook for priests and a guidebook of holy living for the Hebrews. The beginning chapters give detailed instructions for the offering of sacrifices which were to serve as symbols of repentance and obedience. Next come purity laws which discuss what is clean and unclean relative to animals, the period after childbirth, leprosy and the purification after, and purification after bodily discharges. This is followed by instructions for the preparation of the altar and warnings on improper sacrifices and forgiveness of sins (Life Application Bible).

The reader may find it helpful to realize who the Levites were and to be mindful of the power they held within the Hebrew community. They were, indeed, a metaphor for God. Those descendants of the tribe of Levi were the only acceptable members of the priesthood. According to the Bible, Moses was his great grandson. The Levites could only marry within their own tribe, and only to a woman whom had never had sexual relations with another man.

The Levites were considered to be the judges of the law among the Hebrews and the penalty for not following their decisions regarding the law was often death. In Leviticus, there are many references where death is the penalty.

Fire sacrifices were important rituals to the Levites. These were to be made twice daily for a variety of reasons which are recounted in the book of Leviticus for the reader's perusal. The Levites were also assigned the sole rights to eat the animals which were brought for the sacrifices. In Deuteronomy 18: 3-5, we are told:

> And this shall be the priest's due from the
> people, from them that offer a sacrifice, whether
> it be ox or sheep; and they shall give unto the priest
> the shoulder, and the two cheeks and the maw.
> The first fruit also of thy corn, of thy wine,
> and of thine oil, and the first of the fleece of thy
> sheep, shalt thou give him.
> For the Lord thy God hath chosen him out of
> all thy tribes, to stand to minister in the name of the
> Lord, him and his sons for ever.

Thus was born the divine right of the Levite priests. They were also to be given gifts of silver, gold and property as commanded by Yehweh. Numbers 18:20 goes even further to say that they were to be the recipients of every tithe in Israel. In the meantime, every man over twenty was required to give a shekel as ransom for his life to the Levites. While the Levites were precluded from inheriting material wealth from their father, the many commandments in both Numbers and Deuteronomy regarding gifts of privilege assured their wealth and material well being (Stone).

The wealthy and powerful Levites were granted their supreme authority by Moses. In Deuteronomy, Moses completes the writing of the laws and he commands the Levites to place the book of the law beside the Ark of the Covenant as proof that they are in charge. And so it was that the Levites became the law. They owned it and they were the only ones capable of interpreting or changing it, through their own filters, of course. We can draw an interesting parallel here between Judaism and Christianity. In both, we have a message from God, in the former through Moses and the receipt of the ten commandments, and in the latter through Jesus and his message, as found in the Gospels. Then we have man displaying authority over the message, interpreting and changing it as desired. In similar ways, we can compare the role of the Levite priests to that of Paul and the Christian church. We might further conclude that when God and human power over others are synonymously treated through the human condition, the potential for error exists, in direct proportion to the extent of man's filters of irrational thought.

The important thing to be realized, for the moment, is that the ruling class of the Hebrew people were the Levite priests, and that they essentially ruled by divine right. It is with this kind of background knowledge of the priestly class of Levites that the reader might gain greater understanding while continuing to contemplate the book of Leviticus, as well as Numbers and Deuteronomy.

The eighteenth chapter of Leviticus speaks of standards for living which depart from the decadence of Egypt from which they came and also from the decadence of the land of Canaan, to which they go. Much of what is written has to do with the prohibition of sex with family members to include one's own family and the family of one's wife. This also includes thy neighbor's wife, another man and any beast. It is interesting to note that the only code of behavior addressed directly to women is not to lie down with beasts. However, it is Leviticus 18: 22 which is often referenced as God's disapproval of homosexuality in the Old Testament. When taken out of context, this verse says for man not to lie with mankind as with womankind. By reading the entire chapter, however, the reader becomes aware that the obvious inference of most previously given directives, except for the one given to women, is given to married men. The passage seems to have connotations on ownership and taboos within the marriage for the preservation and reverence of the family which is at the very core of Jewish religious life.

It should also be remembered and considered that since 7000 BC, (some say 25,000 BC), long before the time of Moses (1300 BC), and Abraham (1800 BC), the predominant form of religious worship in the Middle East and in many other parts of the world was that of the Goddess religions. Along with the feminine deity dominance came a matrilineal system for the ownership of property. In a material world, inheriting through one's mother tends to render one's father rather powerless. It is easy to understand that men did not like this system any better than women later would like patriarchy. It is pertinent to understand that the ownership of property was indeed a catalyst for change of the deity from the feminine to the masculine gender. The Levite priest would be instrumental in this conversion (Stone). This insight is important to consider as one studies the book of Leviticus.

One finds that Leviticus seems to have a lot to do with ideas regarding what is clean and unclean as it relates to all areas of life, from the Levites' perspective. It would be well for each reader to read the entire book of Leviticus and to also explore the importance of the family in the Jewish tradition to arrive at his or her own conclusions if the reader chooses to ponder this from a literal point of view. It is difficult to do so. It would also be helpful to read *When God Was A Woman* by Merlin Stone and also the work of E.O. James. It should be noted, however, that Leviticus 18: 22 is the primary source reference to the homosexual references which follow in the New Testament.

It is further recommended that the reader study the 20th Chapter of Leviticus, which has to do with the punishments for sin, to realize that having sexual relations with any family member other than one's own spouse was to be punishable by death. This does not seem to have been the case in practice; and while women were bound to fidelity in the marriage (punishable also by death), men were not so bound. We must also remember that the Israelites were told to be fruitful and multiply. In that time, such a law would attempt to insure the preservation of the family unit for procreation purposes. It would also enable the patriarch to track offspring for ownership and inheritance purposes and would, at best, only selectively support the ethical treatment of others.

In this day, the imposition of death to anyone having sexual relations with anyone other than one's own spouse, would most certainly lead to a severe reduction in the world's population. This is not to condone such activity but rather to observe that one lives ethically by inward direction which naturally occurs when one's filters of irrational thought have been removed. It should also be mentioned that initial condemnation of homosexuality may have come about because it did not produce offspring. Such activity would not produce an expansion of ownership nor would it provide for the inheritance of property (through one's father, of course).

As has been previously mentioned, the New Testament references on homosexuality were all written by the Apostle Paul and his religious background and training came from Judaism. The first and most important of the three are found in the first chapter of Romans. For the purpose of giving the reader some background, the book of Romans was Paul's explanation of what the Gospels meant. It examines the message of Jesus from Paul's perspective. Romans was written as a letter to the Christians in Rome to introduce Paul and his message as the authoritative source for the word of God as relayed to the world through the message of Jesus Christ (The Word In Life Study Bible).

Romans was written around 57 AD. Paul had finished his work in the east organizing and establishing the early churches and planned to visit Rome on his way to Spain. In Romans, Paul lays out his opinions on what to believe and how to behave. He did not go to Rome as quickly as intended. When he later arrived at his destination, it is believed that he was killed and martyred there (The Word In Life Study Bible).

The passages most quoted against homosexuality in the New Testament are Romans 1: 26-27. From the King James Version of the Bible, they read as follows:

> For this cause God gave them up to vile affections:
> for even their women did change the natural use into
> that which is against nature:
> And likewise also the men, leaving the natural use
> of the woman, burned in their lust one toward another; men
> with men working that which is unseemly, and receiving in
> themselves that recompense of their error which was meet.

Instead of merely taking these two verses out of context, if the reader looks at what appears before and after them, from a literal point of view, the reader sees the development of an evolving scenario of sin. From Romans 1: 18-32, it can be paraphrased as follows:

1. Man rejects God.

2. God gives man up to worship the beast and defile his nature which leads to homosexuality.

3. This leads to a morally unprincipled mind and fills the individual with unrighteousness and also fills him/her with envy, murder, debate, deceit, malignity and whispers.

4. These are the backbiters, haters of God - whom are despiteful, proud boasters, inventors of evil things and disobedient to parents.

5. They are without understanding, the covenant-breakers and without natural affection, implacable and unmerciful and, last but not least:

6. Those who know God is against such things and still do them, are worthy of death - and not only those who do them, but also those who approve of those who do.

A literal interpretation allows this scenario to imply that one begets the other. Does this make any sense at all? Such thinking is a profound example of irrational thought at work. Such thinking implies that homosexuals are not beings capable of living ethically in their treatment of others and are therefore deserving of judgment. Would Jesus have approved of such an adulteration of his teachings? By reading the Gospels, the reader will find that the answer to this question to be a resounding "No!". A literal interpretation of this translation might further cause one to ask another question: Were Paul's ideas regarding homosexuality a blatant example of homophobia (fear of homosexuality) in the New Testament?

What, exactly, did Paul mean through his writings and more importantly, how is it relevant to the teachings of Jesus as recounted through the gospels? According to Peter J. Gomes in *The Good Book,* Paul was not talking about homosexuality but about the fallen nature of mankind. Whatever Paul's intent, we must be equally cognizant that we receive his message today through the many filters of irrational thought held in the many minds and hearts of those involved in the many translations of his teachings.

The more important questions to be asked are: Does a literal translation of Romans 1: 18-32 have any relationship to the teachings of Jesus as found in the Gospels? Does a literal translation of Romans 1: 18-32 support a loving, non-judgmental attitude for all mankind? Are these verses compassionate? Are they examples of loving your neighbor as yourself? Do they yield an understanding of doing unto others as you would have them do unto you? The ultimate test for Christian validity must always be: does this align with the teachings of Jesus as found in the Gospels? The author encourages each reader to examine these issues for him/herself.

The next reference by Paul is found in Corinthians 6: 9-11. Paul writes this letter to the Corinthians to rein in the church at Corinth. In no uncertain words, he condemns the congregation's divisions over personalities and doctrine and their tolerance for immorality (The Word In Life Study Bible, New Testament Edition). From the King James Version of the Bible, the passages are as follows:

> Know ye not that the unrighteous shall not inherit
> the kingdom of God? Be not deceived: neither
> fornicators, nor idolaters, nor adulterers, nor
> effeminate, nor abusers of themselves with mankind,
> Nor thieves, nor covetous, nor drunkards, nor
> revilers, nor extortioners, shall inherit the kingdom of
> God.
> And such were some of you: but ye are washed, but
> ye are sanctified, but ye are justified in the name of the
> Lord Jesus, and by the Spirit of our God.

Considering a literal interpretation, could the fact that homosexuality is put into this grouping of unethical behaviors again speak of Paul's homophobia? We know that it had nothing to do with the teachings of Jesus, yet it has contributed to a great deal of misunderstanding and judgmental attitudes about homosexuality among many Christian churches. It would seem incompatible for any church to call itself "Christian" and be judgmental against any group of individuals and/or to stand for anything other than the ethical treatment of all others.

The author is not suggesting that the reader throw out the baby with the bath water. Paul was a powerful communicator who is responsible for the formulation of the early church. Where his writings become exponents of the Gospels, they are often quite beautifully communicated; however, he was human and therefore, capable of having his own irrational filters. He also had his own fallible, human agenda which did not align with the Gospels if we are to accept a literal translation. The aspects of his writings which are not based in love for all are based in fear. This is clearly not the message of the Gospels. Sexual orientation is not a personal choice; it is instead a part of one's God given nature, the expression of which can either exalt or depart from the Golden Rule. In this aspect, it is not unlike heterosexuality. Sexuality or sexual orientation is as God created it. The expression of it in ways (homo-or heterosexual) which do not treat others as they would want to be treated is not to be condoned. Expressing sexuality in accordance with the Golden Rule is an ethical principle worthy of adherence by everyone.

The important issue still remains: How does Corinthians 6: 9-11 relate to the Gospels? What did Jesus have to say about inheriting the Kingdom of God, sin and its undoing? Every reader who cares enough to understand must read the Gospels for themselves. A synopsis will not suffice, for this is the essence of the Christian message which, unfortunately, many Christians and Christian churches do not practice. There are also many whom do.

Within the Gospels, the book of Matthew, and more specifically, the Sermon on the Mount, clearly states the teachings of Jesus. The author also suggests as an excellent and adjunct reference source, *The Sermon On The Mount* by Emmet Fox. The reader will then be better able to answer the question: Which exponents of Christianity actually do practice the Christian message? It may be quite surprising to find that many do not.

The last reference Paul makes to homosexuality is found in 1 Timothy 1: 10. In 1 and 2 Timothy, Paul is passing the torch of church leadership to Timothy who is pastor of the church at Ephesus. These letters are basically church organization manuals, the first having to do with the congregation and the second with the pastor. 1 Timothy was written during a time when there were teachers who contradicted Paul's beliefs. He felt that a clear statement of the faith needed to be made to his protégé, Timothy (The Word In Life Study Bible, New Testament Edition).

While verse 10 has little meaning when taken by itself out of context other than to lump fornicators, sodomites, kidnappers, liars and perjurers into the same group, 1 Timothy 1: 1-9 clearly implies there have been teachers who have been teaching in a manner other than the gospel according to Paul and that Timothy should address himself to this problem. The reader may also find it interesting to refer to what Jesus had to say about false teachers in Matthew. Paul says that these teachers do not understand the law, that it is not made for the righteous person but for the ungodly, for sinners, murders, etc. (The Word In Life Study Bible) and in verse 10-11 from the King James Version of the Bible:

> For whoremongers, for them that defile themselves
> with mankind, for menstealers, for liars, for perjured
> persons, and if there be any other thing that is
> contrary to sound doctrine; according to the glorious
> gospel of the blessed God which was committed to
> my trust.

Such disapproval was not unrelated to vestiges of the Goddess religion still thriving in Ephesus.

Through a literal translation, we clearly see that Paul believed his version of the gospel was the only version recognized by God. He felt personally responsible for carrying out God's wishes, believing that his thoughts on the Christian faith were also God's. Again, the only valid question to be asked is: Are Paul's expressions in 1 Timothy in harmony with the teachings of Jesus Christ as recounted in the Gospels. For Christians, acceptance or rejection should be based upon this standard, be it from Paul or from any other religious leader.

One interesting paradox seems to be that while Paul believed that everyone was a sinner, Jesus believed that the purpose of his death was to release mankind from sin. Paul believed that all churches should follow his ideals while perceiving his beliefs and God's as one. Jesus was more concerned that our behavior toward others be devoid of judgment and be loving in nature. In this regard, it would seem that when the messenger becomes the message, there exists great potential for the synergistic expansion of love in the world. When the messenger alters the message, which in any way withholds love from anyone or any group, and does so in the name of righteousness, love is unrighteously diminished.

There is no substitute for each individual Christian reading the Gospels of Matthew, Mark, Luke and John to see how far some churches have strayed from the teachings of Jesus in practice. How surprised Jesus must surely be about the many renditions of theology withholding love in his name which have grown up around his simple and beautiful teachings and which are touted as *the truth, the only truth, so help me God!*

What has been presented for the reader so far is an examination of biblical references on homosexuality from a literal translation of the scriptures. If we knew that every word of the Old and New Testaments were God's and only God's, a literal translation would be meaningful. Because we know that many men took part in this process of recording and revising the *divine truth*, no matter how well intentioned, a literal translation is difficult. It leads one to ask the question: Are holy books best considered as a literal translation of the word of God, or do they make more sense as a metaphorical evocation of the experience of God within us? The latter is commonly accepted in the mystical traditions of both faiths, the Islamic faith and in other mystical religions. Some questions to be asked which might enable one to arrive at acceptable answers are: "Am I able to know more about God through reading and understanding with my cognitive mind or can I know more about God through subjective experience such as prayer and meditation? Am I able to know God better through my mind or through my heart? Is knowing God more like arriving at a scientific truth or more like experiencing a poem? Is knowing God an objective reality or a subjective one? Is knowing God more like reading a description of an ice cream cone or is it more like eating one?"

There may be more validity in accepting a metaphorical interpretation of the Bible or any holy book than there is for a literal interpretation. Just as Edna St. Vincent Millay's love poems are more than the very words themselves and evoke the feeling of love within the reader, holy books have the ability to evoke the experience of God within us. This allows us to feel closer to God. If the Christian reader then allows love to replace fear as the new dispensation that Jesus Christ intended, they learn the message Jesus came to impart. When they allow themselves to become that experience of Christ in the world, they become the message. As they live in the world from that perspective, their lives reflect the Golden Rule, without exclusion, and love multiplies on earth.

If we decide that this way of thinking is just not for us, a metaphorical interpretation is not something that we can accept; only a literal translation will do, then we are faced with another set of circumstances to be reconciled. Which language, which holy book, which translation do we accept as the truth? When our source differs from the other sources, as it surely will, what do we do? Do we consider ours to be right and the others wrong? Which language speaks the truth? Do we embrace the Aramaic, Hebrew, Greek, Latin or

English language? As we travel from one to the other, different words, inferences and meanings will be found as descriptive of the same events. Which holy book do we accept as the authoritative source? Are we even mindful that our holy book has undergone many changes?

For the Jewish individual, the original Aramaic was translated into Hebrew, with the first written text emerging between 1300 - 165 BC, which became the Septuagint, translating the Hebrew into Greek and written between 250 - 50 BC. Later texts were edited between the 7th and 9th centuries AD. Was anything changed between then and 1488 AD. when the Hebrew text was first printed (The World's Great Religions)? And, what about the Dead Sea Scrolls discovered in this century which are believed to date back to 140 BC? The evidence here is not yet concluded except perhaps from a Catholic perspective. What about the work of Dr. Barbara Thiering of Sydney University in Australia, noted Dead Sea Scrolls scholar, who disagrees with the date of 140 BC and puts forth their time as being contemporary with the life of Jesus? Her ideas would change religion as we know it. How the Dead Sea Scrolls might change the nature and meaning of our holy book source, especially for Christians, is a question not yet answered.

The first New Testament sources were the texts written in Greek on papyrus and leather between 50 - 100 AD. In 325 AD, Constantine organized the Council of Nicea for the purpose of creating a union between church and state. History would later prove such a relationship to be horrific. This council established the position of Jesus Christ as God. It is interesting to note Jesus Christ was proclaimed God through the political process. It also necessitated that historical documents be changed to better support the church's position. In 389 AD, the Alexandria library would be burned and subsequent councils would further alter original doctrine.

After the Council of Nicea, we have the next texts completed in 350 AD and in 400 AD, we have St. Jerome's Vulgate becoming the authoritative Catholic Bible. This was a Latin translation from Greek texts which was later translated into the Donquay and later, the Confraternity, which is the U.S. Catholic version printed in 1952. Protestants should also be aware of the evolution of their holy book. From St. Jerome's Vulgate comes the Wycliffe's Bible, which was the first English translation around 1382 AD. It evolved into the Tyndale, the Great Bible, the Geneva and the King James. From it came the Algonquin Bible for the American Indians and finally, the newest of the U.S. Protestant bible evolved known as the Revised Standard Version of 1952 (The World's Great Religions).

The question is: Which man's version of holy books is also God's version? When we begin to ask such a question, we see some of the problems involved in accepting a literal translation of any holy book as the literal word of God. However, we can clearly maintain that all holy books have the potential to evoke the experience of God within us so that we might live our lives as an example of that experience. From that perspective, all of them are the *divine word of God*.

God's word is a living, breathing thing, forever applicable to every culture in every time. The written form of it has been dynamic and ever changing throughout history so that men and women, who also are changing, can understand, relate, become inspired and learn from it. If we believe that God's teaching has only to do with the mere understanding of words written by man about God and nothing to do with receiving an inner experience of God and living from that perspective, do we not miss the point? The thing that really matters is: Do we treat our neighbor as ourselves? Rabbi Akava taught this mitzvah as the great principle of the Torah, and Jesus proclaimed it to be the most important of his teachings, as do the other great religions of the world.

A literal translation of a holy book seems to give man more power than God. The author uses the word "man" on purpose as only men were instrumental in the various changes through which the current holy books evolved and, indeed, in both, Judaism and Christianity. This, in itself, is interesting and we shall continue to address the issue of gender as this text evolves. Nevertheless, it seems pertinent to now ask the question: "Is it logical to give man's words, which continue to change, more importance than the experience of God in our lives?" A person who adheres to a literal translation of any holy book may be doing exactly that. This can create a diversion which can only inhibit the receiving of God's message of love for all and therefore, its practice in the world.

It is important for each reader to decide from which vantage point they shall view the holy books, literally or metaphorically. It is also important for each individual to read enough appropriate material to arrive at their own informed opinion. It is not enough to rely solely upon a rabbi, priest or minister's opinion or upon the dogma and doctrine which influences their opinions. These have changed throughout history and they are subject to change again. However, the core upon which religious truths are based has not changed. The ten commandments have remained the core for Judaism and the teachings of Jesus, as recounted in the Gospels, have remained the core for Christianity. They are the Golden Rule. Knowing the beliefs and opinions of one's faith is important but looking at them in a larger context is essential for arrival at one's own personal truth.

Homosexuals and those whom judge them have tended to shy away from familiarity with the references on homosexuality which appear in holy books. Those whom judge them have wrongfully used selective passages of holy books to justify their own prejudices. Parents and friends of gays and lesbians also tend to be shy of information that would lead them to the practice of truth, as they love and support their homosexual relatives and friends. Religious leaders can and should take the lead in the revolution which would restore love to all. It is the lesson of love, without exclusion, which all of us are here to learn.

It is time to become well informed on these issues as well as the nature of the core message of all the great religions of the world. A compassionate code of behavior which inspires everyone to treat others as they would be treated is that message. Each individual's behavior in the world provides the medium for that message to be actualized.

Our progress on this path is quite evident through our behavior toward others. All that we do displays what we have learned or failed to learn about this message. Perhaps Confucius said it best in his Analects when he said: "The man who both practices what he preaches and preaches what he practices knows heaven." If we would grow in the expression of God's love, it is important to open our eyes and to recognize the individuals and religious institutions who emulate these ideals through their actions in the world and to leave behind those whom do not.

REFLECTIONS

Mother-Father Source of my being, help me to pursue my own personal truth through the contemplation of man's holy books to learn of his quest to understand You through the written word. Help me to go beyond that limited, cerebral understanding to the more complete experience of You in my heart.

Thank you Mother-Father Source of my being, for granting me my greatest wish: that I might have the experience of You now, that I might feel Your love, peace and joy within me now, so totally and so completely that I am able to do none other than to express it in the world. Help me to live my life as Your expression as I willingly step aside and allow You to see with my eyes, hear with my ears, speak with my mouth, think with my mind and love with my heart.

Help me Mother-Father Source of my being, to release my judgment against others that they might learn to release theirs against me, so that the two of us might rise, more fully, to what we are and know that what we are is love. Arriving here, there is compassion for all. Allow me to behold and to create, through my own example, a world where everyone is ready to treat all others as they would be treated, to create a world where love at last replaces fear.

CHAPTER THREE

Goddess / God And Religion Are Not The Same

Goddess/God and religion seem to have existed in some form throughout history. The earliest examples are found in the Goddess religions. Later came the male dominated religions. For some time, they existed side by side, and we know that the male dominated form of religion did caste aspersions upon the female form. Moses was very concerned about the Canaanites, their beliefs and their methods of worship. They were called pagan and heathen (non-Jewish and therefore, having no religion). This criticism was strongly directed at the Goddess religion. History tells us that the male dominated religions did finally win the battle. After the year 500 AD, there were few strong vestiges of the Goddess religion to be found. After thousands of years, the balance of power had finally shifted from one gender to the other.

Humankind seems to have always realized a power greater than self. While the form has changed many times, as is exemplified by the many religions and sects within them, the voice of the Source of all good has usually been initially experienced as a subjective experience through the mind and heart of one human being. History tells us that the Goddess was revered long before God was revealed to Moses and the prophets of the Old Testament, to the Buddha, Lao Tzu, Jesus Christ and others. All of these great teachers were inspired by a personal experience of the Power greater than self. The evidence we have of these master teachers exist for us as mental images through the written word.

Until we allow them to move from our minds to inspire our hearts with love, we are dealing with only half a truth. This opens the way for false ideas to be confused as the truth. An example of this might be: "I love God with all of my heart and I hate homosexuals" (women, blacks, abortion doctors and/or any other group). The latter is but a false idea which only serves to lessen the former. It limits the amount of love one is able to feel for God. It says: "I love you God but I hate what you created". Contemplate, for a moment, what is wrong with this picture.

Hating homosexuals or any other group clearly serves as a barrier to love of God and withholding love in God's name only serves to increase that barrier. For the maligned and hated group to also hate right back is just as unproductive for the obvious reasons. Retaliative behavior only takes on the barrier to love, personalizes it and sails it back. The author suggests that removing the barrier might be a better course of action.

Love is the only energy that can heal this condition and it is called into action when one entity refuses to hate. Someone must simply stop the cycle of abuse. The love which can be generated from that action helps the other entity to heal and this is how the barrier is removed. Once this happens, love can flow and fill the space between them. This is the principle behind the effectiveness of non-violence. One can begin by simply recognizing that everyone is trying to overcome and to remove their barriers to love, even though it does not always look that way. Taking this mental idea to heart can begin to halt the barrier-increasing process within us. This will eventually enable us to move that knowledge from our minds to our hearts. In doing so, we shall then be able to deal with the whole truth, and not just half of it. The great teachers of the world have all been able to touch us with this truth through their example.

The primary reason we continue to revere the master teachers of the past is because we realize that they experienced the Source of their being through both their minds and their hearts, and in so doing, they became examples of the message of love through their ethical treatment of others. This is what a great master is, a profound *example* of goodness. Learning to do likewise is our heart's aspiration. When we learn this completely through doing it, the illusion of fear of anyone or anything must become the expression of love for all. No longer choosing to be separated, we are one. So far, it would appear that humankind has made more progress with the mind than with the heart.

In dealing from the mind's perspective, it is interesting to note that society seems to become very much like its definition of God. If we turn to the New College Edition of the *American Heritage Dictionary*, we find an uncapitalized version which defines god as "a being of supernatural powers or attributes, believed in and worshipped by a people; especially, a male deity thought to control some part of nature or reality or to personify some force or activity." A capitalized version of God is defined as: "A being conceived as the perfect, omnipotent, omniscient originator and ruler of the universe, the principle object of faith and worship in monotheistic religions."

To paraphrase in the vernacular, one could say that the major "One God" religions, those being Judaism, Christianity and Islam, perceive God as an all powerful male know-it-all who created the universe and serves as its CEO. This is further reinforced by its definition in the female gender. The word goddess appears only in the uncapitalized form and is defined as: "1. A female deity. 2. A woman of great beauty or grace. 3. A woman adored as a deity." Here we find the female aspect unequally venerated and presented more as the object of man's affection. It seems valid to conclude that assignation of the male gender to God has created a patriarchal system for religion and society as did the viewing of the Source of our being as female create a matriarchal system in the days of the Goddess religion. It is the nature of patriarchy to create inequity for the female gender just as was the case in reverse for matriarchy.

The question is: Who assigned gender to the power in the universe greater than ourselves as we know it to be? Was it God or was it mankind? The author shall provide one very important clue: It probably was not God. This error was further reinforced by religious leaders along the way as evidenced by Jewish men being commanded to thank God during their morning prayers for not making them Gentiles, slaves or women. The acceptance of any belief which serves to separate oneself from others can only serve as a barrier to love.

In Christianity, Paul's establishment of the early church in the male tradition of authority, as he had experienced through his upbringing as a Jew, and Augustine's addition to it through his *Confessions*, which espoused the denigration of sexuality and women (Armstrong), did not help matters. Ideas which in any way construe that one gender is preferential to the other is demeaning to the entire human race. Gender preference is but one more way to construct a barrier to love.

In addition to the spiritual disenfranchisement of women in Judaism, Christianity and Islam, assigning gender to God also implies ideas of sexuality as man begins to envision God as himself. Once he creates a personal God like himself, it follows that he would naturally project his own sexual repressions, guilt and taboos upon the deity. This enables him to experience them as God's. *Such is divine projection.* How else could he endeavor to withhold love in God's name? Likewise, it might be expected that homosexuality would be more opposed in patriarchal religions by religious leaders whom are predominantly male, and the opposition of this minority should then be greater by the males of their congregations than by their female members. This seems to be the case in the world today.

Assigning a gender to God attempts to throw God off balance and creates sexism in the world. A patriarchal religion withholds love and equality for women. In reverse, this was perhaps as true in the days of the Goddess religions when the deity was viewed from the point of reference of the female gender. Going from one extreme to another is often a natural human foible, after which balance finds its way to middle ground. Going from a matriarchal based religious society to a patriarchal one is such an extreme. It is time that we find balance in our perception of the power in the universe which is greater than ourselves. That Power is not only male or female. It is both and more, just as we are. The Source of our being is, indeed, androgynous and would find no barriers to love based upon gender. While Goddess/God and religion are not the same, the way that we perceive the Source will dictate the form of our religion as well as some of our prejudices.

An interesting example has been the exclusion of women serving as clergy since the beginning of the patriarchal religions. While there are many sexist ideas put forth in God's name, is it rational to believe that the Source of all good is sexist? One might begin to make better sense of patriarchy if one views it against what came before it. Here we would find the Goddess religions, matrilineal ownership of property and a matriarchal society where only those of the female gender were suitable as priestesses, and where the Power in the universe greater than ourselves was considered to be female. Would men not feel oppressed and powerless in such a world? Would it be unusual for these men to then become the oppressors and the ones in authority with God? Is this not exactly how the pattern of abuse works?

Long before any of the major religions about which we know, there existed the Goddess religion. Remnants of it date back to 25,000 BC. Long before patriarchy there existed matriarchy. One can see how easily retaliation might have come about: "You did it to me and I shall do it right back to you". Whether it is completely true or not, as might be found through a conclusive burden of proof, there is wisdom in accepting such a premise. Society can then move on and can discontinue calling 911 on the many issues which serve as its barriers to love.

There is no argument which denies the clergy to women that is not sexist. Sexism is a major barrier to love. While religious leaders debate the issue, the Gospel of Thomas has some interesting things to say. This gospel was lost for 16 centuries and discovered in upper Egypt in 1945. It is an anthology of the sayings of Jesus and considered one of the earlier manuscripts related to the New Testament. It is believed to have been written during the time of Jesus and translated into Greek in about 140 AD. Some of the passages are especially interesting with regard to the issue of gender.

Simon Peter wants Mary to leave the group of disciples because he believes that women are not worthy of the religious life. In response, Jesus says that he will make her male so that she also will become a living spirit resembling them. Jesus further states that every woman who makes herself male will enter the Kingdom of Heaven. (A. Guillaumont et.al.) What, exactly does he mean by this?

We know that Jesus liked to speak in parables. If we consider that Simon Peter's belief is that maleness equates to being worthy of God, we might envision and imagine Jesus' response to be as follows: "I shall make her as worthy in her own eyes as you are in yours, that she too may become a living spirit, resembling you males in your belief of your worthiness. For every woman who believes herself to be worthy, will enter the Kingdom of Heaven." It is probable that this may have been what Jesus meant. Whatever the exact meaning of this passage was, we know that sexism was not the intent. Not only does it not align with the Gospels, sexism would speak of an irrational Creator.

We can let this realization and this gospel become the catalyst for the first step in the elimination of sexism in religions and for hastening the ordination of women in all religious faiths. Let the second step become the creation of a Power in the universe greater than ourselves which is not limited, in any way, to any one gender. Since the nature of each individual is both masculine and feminine, let us stop denying half of whom we are in the worship of our Creator and in the institutions which serve to celebrate the Power greater than ourselves. Finding balance within ourselves and our religious organizations will help us to begin to treat others as we would be treated.

In America and Europe, it is easy to mistake the monotheistic religions as being predominant in the world; however, the contrary is true. The Far Eastern religions are numerically greater in practitioners than those of Christianity, according to Hans-Joachim Schoeps in *The Religions of Mankind.*

The numbers for Christianity have been declining and continue to do so amid much controversy among religious leaders in their abuse of power and their failure to practice the message they impart. We have clearly seen this through various financial frauds, sexual escapades and pedophilia problems of many Christian religious leaders of the 1980s and 90s. While such events speak of blatant misuse of public trust and unethical behavior, humanity becomes more and more disillusioned with their religious leaders.

Many Christians are also distanced from their faith because of some of the problems a Creator of one gender creates. It is the author's opinion that one need not throw away the deity because man creates an ungodly form for its expression. One need only change the name and seek a form (or create a new one) which is compatible, without exception, to the great truth of all faiths known as the Golden Rule. An ethical life always treats others, all others, as we would be treated. In examining some of the other religions which do not exclusively praise or assign the male gender to a personal God, we find that Hinduism is the oldest of such religions.

Hinduism had its beginnings many years before Moses, Buddha or Christ walked the earth. Its formal beginning dates to 1500 - 800 BC. in India with the writing of its holy book called the Vedas, which consist of four different texts, and the Upanishads, which are believed to contain hidden wisdom for the training of disciples and priests. Together, they are referred to as Vedanta. They emphasize knowledge through contemplation which leads to union with God, which is called Brahman. It is the union of Atman with Brahman, the human soul with the world spirit, which is salvation. Such is achieved through insight. This mystical tradition relies on subjective experience of God for the experience of oneness with all things. Once achieved, the individual is free from the endless cycle of rebirths (Schoeps).

Hinduism differs from Judaism and Christianity by having no specific dogmas and it results in much greater religious tolerance. The union of Atman with Brahman is reached through prayer, meditation and also through a life of purity, self-control, detachment, truth, nonviolence, charity and compassion for all creatures. Brahman is contemplated in the old scriptures as being woman, man and all things.

Because the Hindus see the Creator in all things, they have great reverence for life in all forms. The principle of ahimssa represents this through nonviolence to animals as well as humans. This is why religious Hindus are vegetarians. To kill an animal for food would be against their religious beliefs. Because Hindus believe in karma, every act has a moral significance. Life is without beginning and without end. "As one does, so one becomes", is a circular view of, "Do unto others as you would have them do unto you" (The World's Great Religions). The Hindu beliefs embrace the Golden Rule through action in the world. An exception to this is found in the concept of the caste system to which one is born. One's caste fixes one's duties and responsibilities; however, the modern constitution of India makes it a criminal offense to discriminate against anyone based upon caste, color or creed (The World's Great Religions).

The contemporary evolution of Hinduism as experienced in the west dates back to 1897 with Vivekananda establishing the Ramakrishna Mission. His noble goal was the non-dogmatic union of all religions. He believed that by different roads, all sought the same God. Christianity has much to learn from the religious tolerance of this view. Vivekananda's ideas, which continue to be carried forward through Vedanta Centers all over the world, have influenced the Theosophical Society and some of the later metaphysical movements and religions in America. The basic recognition is that there are many paths to God and they are all respected. Seeking God is more important than the vehicle one uses while doing so.

Some of the beliefs of Hinduism which have influenced religious faiths currently in practice deserve a careful look. While avoiding a patriarchal, gendered God, they are more tolerant of other religions. They are less dogmatic and judgmental of others and their message is based in love instead of fear. At the very least, it would be educational to the reader to visit different groups and churches to experience other versions of religious thought to evaluate their personal meaning first hand. The author does not imply that these groups are branches of Hinduism as such, but that they are influenced by some of its important beliefs.

It would be broadening for the reader to go on a religious odyssey which includes visits to a Vedanta Center, a Theosophical Society meeting, a Christian Science church, a Unity church, a church of Religious Science, a Science of Mind church, a Quaker meeting house or other less traditional and/or non-denominational churches to see how it feels and to experience where it might lead you. If it should lead you closer to the experience of God in your life by helping you to remove your barriers to love, Hallelujah! If not, seek elsewhere. Remember, we have been told to seek and we shall find.

Become a seeker until you find a way to express love for everyone and all things. Arriving here you will know that, at last, you have found a rational Power and the true Source of all good within you. You cannot help but become its expression in the world. You and your religion will then become synergistic in the world and you will begin to teach what you are through your fine example. Your religion will spiritually support you in your quest to express the goodness of the Source of all good in the world as you remove your prejudicial barriers to love. There will no longer be room inside you to hate anyone or any group.

Another religion older than Christianity by some five and one half centuries is Buddhism. It spread from the island of Ceylon to Japan and throughout large sections of Asia. It is believed that there may be more than 500 million practitioners of Buddhism (Schoeps).

Buddha himself left no written word. His message was handed down through oral transmission much like the teachings of Jesus. They were not written down until two and one-half centuries after his death; however, according to Hans-Joachim Schoeps, there were less discrepancies in Buddha's work from the oral to written form than there are differences between the Aramaic, which was the language of Jesus, and the first Greek translation of the Gospels.

Buddhism is based upon the teachings of a man named Siddhartha Gautama who became the Buddha (the Enlightened One). He lived during the 6th century BC. which was also the time of Confucius in China and some of the prophets of the Old Testament. His foundation for the human spirit consisted of four noble truths. They spoke of suffering as being universal and craving as the cause of suffering. Only by overcoming craving will we cease to suffer. The way to be free from craving is found through following the Eightfold Path. It is the way to achieve Nirvana. Concentration and meditation are tools for application. Schoeps compares them to the use of prayer in Christian mysticism. This enables one to arrive at Nirvana, which marks the end of the cycle of rebirth. Nirvana is a state of bliss where there is only peace and total indifference to all pleasure and pain.

The steps on the Eightfold Path are: 1. Right knowledge 2. Right intention 3. Right speech 4. Right conduct 5. Right means of livelihood 6. Right effort 7. Right mindfulness 8. Right concentration. By following this path, the individual arrives at Nirvana and is free at last from the wheel of rebirth (Schoeps).

If this sounds like Hinduism, it is no accident. Buddha had been a Hindu. He accepted the doctrine of reincarnation and karma but he disapproved of the caste system held in esteem by the Hindus because he believed in everyone's equality and spiritual potential (The World's Great Religions).

There are two schools of thought in Buddhism. Hinayama Buddhism is followed by southern Asians and seeks salvation through individual austerity. Mahayana Buddhism is followed in China, Japan, Korea, Tibet and Mongolia and seeks salvation by faith and good works. Both forms of Buddhism embrace the noble Eightfold Path as the means to the end, the practice of which leads to peace of mind for the individual and good works in the world (The World's Great Religions). Is this not but another version of the Golden Rule?

Rather than revering the Buddha as a deity, he is looked on as a wonderful man who deeply understood the mysteries of life. This is probably the way we would look at Jesus today had it not been for the political and religious convention of the 4th century mandated by Emperor Constantine. The gathering was called the Council of Nicea. It claimed that Jesus Christ was both fully God and fully man. We should remain mindful that it was indeed mortal men making this proclamation and arriving at this truth. It would unite church and state in such a way that would permit politics to join religion in becoming synergistic in the creation of barriers to love. The perpetuation of this activity would continue onward and it would later reveal some of the darkest periods in the history of mankind. It seems somewhat paradoxical that Nicea would later become the first Muslim city to be captured during the Crusades. The Hindus and the Buddhists would probably explain it as karma.

Buddhism spread because it held high ideals of right conduct and right treatment of others: tolerance; nonviolence; respect for all individuals; love of animals; nature and all there is. The monotheistic religions have much to learn from this noble faith.

The two most popular Buddhist sects in Japan are Shin and Zen. Shin is the largest and Zen is the most familiar in the West. It espouses a life of plain living and meditation by its followers. Zen is more closely aligned with Hinayana Buddhism in southern Asia. The Zen Buddhists depend upon years of disciplined meditation to bring a flash of enlightenment (The World's Great Religions). Zen is a mystical religion where the experience of God is subjective, much like the mystics of the monotheistic religions such as the Jewish Kabbalists, the Islamic Sufis and the Christian Mystics.

Confucianism, Buddhism and Taoism are all important to the development of religious experience in China. Confucianism is a system of ethics. Buddhism is the most formalized religion of the three and Taoism is a form of mysticism taught by Lao Tzu. The Chinese considered them to be three roads to the same destination (The World's Great Religions).

Taoism has less to do with morals than it has to do with seeking balance. Lao Tzu did have his version of the Golden Rule: "I do good to those who do me good, and to those that do not do me good I also do good - and thus, it is well with everyone" (Schoeps). The Tao means the way or the law of life. Implicit therein is the interaction of yang and yin, heaven and earth. From this, all things come into being. Both are necessary to the order of the universe. When they are in harmony, all is well. Lao Tzu taught that if we lived by the Tao, we would live a natural and a simple life. We would not be ambitious for power and there would be no war, for all would feel and express brotherly love (The World's Great Religions). Taoists are the opposite of Western control freaks. Their motto is: do nothing, allow things to take their natural course without interference. All that is antithetical to the Tao will perish. The West would have much to gain from considering the Tao.

Lao Tzu was born in 604 BC and Confucius in 551 BC. They are the two most important sages of China. Confucius considered himself a teacher, not a creator or a deity. He agreed with Lao Tzu regarding the Tao. He taught simple and practical rules for daily living from which came the Chinese system of ethics. It was based upon the belief of the basic goodness of everyone and upon honesty (The World's Great Religions).   "The superior man makes honesty the foundation of his existence" (Analects). When asked if there were any one application to be acted upon daily, the answer was: "Never do to others what you would not like them to do to you" (Analects).

In glancing at some of the major religions which do not assign one gender to the Power in the universe greater than ourselves and which are not personal (God taking on man's qualities), we find a common core of agreement in all religions on the right treatment of all others through the adherence to the Golden Rule. We know that they have not always succeeded in practicing them but the intent is there within the beliefs embraced. We also found this to be true of the monotheistic religions recounted in Chapter 2, even though we are also aware that they have not always been practiced. Treating others as we would be treated is the greatest spiritual truth by which we can live. We can easily draw the conclusion that this one principle is in harmony with the intent of all major religions of the world. God has similarly inspired humankind throughout the planet with this one simple truth. This is **The Truth** of all religions which so many individuals fail to practice. There is no group more aware of this than homosexuals. Barriers to love against them is society's most extreme form of prejudice.

To judge and to hate any individual for the way they were created is to judge and to hate the Creator. Zealots of prejudice, from religious and non-religious groups, substitute unethical behavior for the Golden Rule as they persecute others because they are different from themselves.

One reason that they do so is because their irrational ideas have allowed them to believe that all homosexuals engage in unrighteous behavior, such as forcing others to have sex with them, taking advantage of children, killing their partner in a domestic dispute, etc. The vast majority of gays and lesbians know that nothing could be further from the truth. In fact, there is a much higher proportionate incidence of sexual and physical abuse within the heterosexual population.

Because homosexuals tend to live secretly in fear (in the closet), the rest of the population is unable to realize that most of them are honorable and ethical human beings whom greatly contribute to the world. Zealots count upon this silence to perpetuate and strengthen their message of hate. It will not be nullified until gays and lesbians refuse to live in fear for who they are and insist upon being known and evaluated by their ethical treatment of others through their practice of the Golden Rule. The point is simply this: if society knows whom the homosexuals are, they would surely know that the majority of homosexuals are ethical human beings. Those whom are not ethical should answer to the same standards as everyone else.

To illustrate, when we read an article in the newspaper about a father brought to justice for sexually abusing his children, we are indeed saddened to learn of such unethical treatment but we do not automatically assume that all fathers sexually abuse their children. We do not do so because we know many kind and loving fathers who treat their children well. When we read an article about gay sensationalism of any sort, the conclusion tends to be that all gays and lesbians are like the horror stories about which we read. This is a perfectly natural conclusion if one does not know any homosexuals whom would prove it otherwise. Not only has choosing to live "in the closet" perpetuated much pain for homosexuals, it has also inhibited the rest of society from healing their homosexual prejudice. Humanity can and will heal its prejudice as homosexuals help them to do so by revealing who they are. This will help human beings to see that there is no need for exclusion of homosexuals in their practice of the Golden Rule.

The most frightening part of this failure to practice the Golden Rule and general intolerance for any point of view other than their own is found among the fundamentalist sects of the patriarchal and monotheistic religions. Fundamentalism could easily be called anti-God because their behavior is often selectively devoid of love and compassion. It is often politics masquerading as religion, aggression explaining itself as righteousness and hate creating a poor impersonation of love. Compassion is often replaced by commitment to their agenda. It is a "my way or death's highway" approach to life. Fundamentalists give lip service to Yahweh, Christ and Allah while doing ungodly things in his name. It is the Jewish fundamentalists and the Muslim fundamentalists who engage in unholy behavior and call it a Holy War. The West Bank and Gaza Strip problems seem to be more about intolerance than about love.

As bad, or worse, are the Christian fundamentalists who shoot abortion doctors as they redefine "Thou shalt not kill" to suit their own agenda. And what about *Christian Family Values*? Has this term become a mask for the dissemination of hatred for gays and lesbians? As Armstrong has noted, fundamentalism, in all forms, is a reductive faith, a retreat from God and should be rejected as inauthentic.

The politicians of our country should take note of the use and abuse of religious power through political forums throughout history to revisit the reasons why our founding fathers established separation of church and state. In the last half of the 20th century, and more specifically, during the Reagan presidency, we somehow lost our minds in this regard. This was evidenced by the Moral Majority's profound political power. The Christian Coalition and other conservative religious groups presented similar masks in 1996. They are religious entities with a political agenda which would create more barriers to love by withholding love and perpetuating hate in the name of God. This is not the Christian ideal.

When religion becomes political, it shows that it cares more about power over others than it does about love of God. Politicians would do well to refuse to accept financial support from any religious organization or institution. Such action would ensure that the political far right would not become the forum for a fundamentalist religious agenda. Instead, we have seen the example of the Republican presidential candidate in 1996 returning a donation to his campaign from a gay Republican political organization. This action can only be viewed as one of appeasement to the religious right.

Such actions must be viewed for what they imply, a candidate in debt to a religious agenda. This only strengthens everyone's awareness of the religious right's involvement in the political process. Many would abandon political support of such candidates. Loving people with a greater concern for codes of political conduct which reflect fairness for all and which do not attempt to judge others should not be under estimated.

Abortion and homosexuality are the hot issues on the fundamentalists' bandwagon. They masquerade as *Right to Life* and *Family Values.* Right to lifers confuse the soul with the body as they employ their Christian-Crusades mentality to claim their rights to the body of every woman. This could only happen in a patriarchal society where God is male. We must never forget that the spoken ideal of the Christian Crusades was to liberate the Christians in the name of God. The fact that the methodology was to kill others, and eventually each other when there was material gain to be realized, is often forgotten.

Those who espouse *Family Values* often use it as a veil for homosexual prejudice. Homosexuals pose no threat to anyone's family. Domestic violence does. Why is their energy not used in this direction? Could it be that in a patriarchal religion and society, the perpetrators of domestic violence tend to be predominately male?

Fundamentalists are the modern day "Crusaders". They are prepared to do ungodly things in God's name. If we use the Gospels as our standard for evaluation, we find that the speech and actions of Fundamentalists in the world is often un-Christian and ungodly, for it is devoid of love for humankind.

Christian fundamentalists seek to exert their will upon women, gays and lesbians through legislation in the political arena. They would depose God to sit in judgment on their brothers and sisters. In their discrimination against women and homosexuals, Christian fundamentalism becomes the most restrictive girdle that man has ever imposed on God and the most profound extreme of ungodly oppression among the patriarchal religious forms.

Politicians and their constituents would be better served to realize this and know that their acceptance of financial support from such religious groups and individuals is the only way to give power to these ideas in the world. Supporting these ideas will, sooner or later, contribute to their downfall. Learning the wisdom of separation of church and state could be learned through the exclusion of religious contributions, overtly and covertly, by all politicians until we develop loving hearts without barriers to love.

Goddess/God and religion are not the same! The Source of our being is the Power and religion is humanity's created form for communication with that Power on earth. There is one Power, inclusive of and beyond both genders, and there are many created forms. It is interesting to note that many individuals give up embracing the Power greater than themselves simply because they disagree with the form. This is not logical nor is it necessary. There are many forms from which to choose and one standard by which to

evaluate them. There are many paths to Goddess/God and one Golden Rule.
Does it make sense to say: "I am not going to Miami because I do not want to
ride in this car." If it is important to go to Miami, why not consider another
mode of transportation?

If you are not happy about your vehicle on your journey to your
Source, do not abandon the journey because of the vehicle. Go shopping for a
vehicle that feels right for you and expresses you to the fullest. Shop for your
faith, church or spiritual support system, at least, as diligently as you shop for
your automobile. Shop with a standard for evaluation. Just as you would ask:
"How many miles to the gallon?", try asking: "How does this faith, this
church, this group attempt to practice the Golden Rule?" In arriving at your
decision, it may help to look less at what is said and more at what is done, for
actions speak the truth. No, Goddess/God and religion are not the same. The
Source is the Power in the universe greater than ourselves and religions are the
many roads which mankind has paved to the Mother-Father Source. There is
one that is right for you.

The Source can be your wonderful partner in life if you refuse to allow
the inconsistencies of religion to get in the way. Affirming the Source in your
life does not require a formal religion although one certainly can support it if
you seek and find one that makes "works" as important as "faith". With or
without religion, the visible proof that you affirm the Source in your life is
thoroughly transparent and easily shown by the way you treat others. Do you
do unto others as you would have them do unto you? This is **The Way**, the
peaceful and the loving way home.

REFLECTIONS

Mother-Father Source of my being, I dedicate myself to healing everything within me that would stand in my way from living a life which adheres completely and passionately to the Golden Rule. I reflect upon those moments when I missed the mark and I give them all to You. I forgive myself for these errors and, where I can seek the forgiveness of those I have harmed by my mistakes, I willingly do so. I am grateful for Your help as I go forward to cancel out my errors of the past through forgiveness.

Forgive me, Mother-Father Source of my being, for any wrong perceptions I have held about You. Whatever they have been, they have had their value in getting me this far. For this, I am grateful but I desire to go further now. Inspire me to know You more deeply with my heart and lead me where You will, that I might know and trust you more.

Help me to know that You and religion are not the same and help me to see You, and all of the forms which try to contain You, more clearly. Help me to make decisions which support Your living presence in my life through my behavior in the world.

CHAPTER FOUR

You And The Source Of Your Being

Your relationship with the Source of your being is a very personal matter. It is an issue which must make sense to you to be personally acceptable. It does not matter that it does not make sense to others. It is not strengthened or weakened by arguing about it, nor does it need to be justified or vindicated in anyone else's eyes. It is enough that it is yours and you are unique in all this world. Your perception of the Source is where your relationship begins.

The way you see Goddess/God has to influence what you see in the world. Do you see God as male? If you use the word "God", of course you do; the name itself implies it. Before you discount this as feminist nonsense, close your eyes and say a prayer substituting the word "Goddess" for God and see how this feels to you. Many individuals will find this difficult. Now, try to picture what your version of God looks like. Do you see a dress and makeup or do you see a wise old man with a long white beard? This little exercise will lead you to the truth within yourself. Are you sexist in relation to God? The truth will be found in your visualization. If you use the word "God" to describe the Power greater than yourself, you may tend to associate the male gender with power, real deity power, that is. Contemplate, for a moment, what many people thinking this one thought might create in the world. Now open your eyes and see what it looks like. Well, what do you think? This is it!

If life is a poker game and you are male, you are holding four aces. If you are female, your hand looks more like a pair of tens. So, what is the solution here; should we then pray to the Goddess? Indeed, many women have become disillusioned with the male God. To validate themselves, they have turned back to the Earth Mother, the Goddess, who reigned alone as deity long before the God of Abraham. While there are many who would like to believe that the world began with the Bible, we know that the Goddess religions preceded the God of Abraham by thousands of years. What was she like? How and why did things change?

51

We have archaeological confirmation that the earliest known government, medicine, agriculture, architecture, wheeled vehicles, ceramics, textiles and written language were developed in societies that worshipped the female deity. The Goddess was known by many names, depending upon the location. She was called: Astarte, Inanna, Nut, Nana, Anat, Istar, Isis, Au Set, Ishara, Ashtart, Attoret, Attar, Hathor and many others. In the Old Testament, she is known as the despised pagan deity, Ashtoreth. She was also known as the Great Goddess, the Divine Ancestress and the Queen of Heaven (Stone).

The Goddess was revered as the Earth Mother. It was an easy conclusion at which to arrive since it was clearly apparent that it was the female who gave birth to new life. Initially, man's role in the process was probably not realized as it was nine months later when the baby arrived. Because the female was the purveyor of life, it was natural for the deity to assume the female gender.

Along with this power came ownership of property. Land descended through the female line and women also became the chief producers of food. They discovered how to cultivate the land for the production of crops. Controlling the land, the food supply and the perpetuation of the species, they held both earthly and divine power. Whenever anyone closed their eyes to pray, they clearly saw a dress and make-up.

History tells us that, at first, the Goddess appears to have ruled alone. Mythology tells us that she had a son or brother who became her lover. It was this young male who was symbolized in the ritual of sexual union with the Goddess. This male was known by various names, depending upon the country and the language. Known as Damuzi, Tammuz, Attis, Adonis, Osiris or Baal, legend has it that he died in his youth. This created an annual period of grief among those who worshipped the Goddess. Examples of similar beliefs were widespread and unify the worshippers of the Goddess. Such a legend was known in Egypt by 3000 BC. It was also found in Sumer, Babylon, Anatolia and Canaan. It was evidenced in the Greek legend of Aphrodite and Adonis and in pre-Christian Rome through the legends of Cybele and Attis (Stone).

As invaders came from the North, attacking and conquering cities where the Goddess was worshipped, these Indo-Europeans brought their own warrior and/or father god with them. They then imposed him upon the conquered cities. The evidence for archaeological and historical placement in time is around 2400 BC. (Stone).

As the invasions and conquests of cities continued, we had the situation of the unconquered cities worshipping a female deity and the conquered ones worshipping a male deity. Often the cities existed side by side. Instead of merging both deities, the situation remained an either/or proposition.

It is quite probable that the male god of these northern invaders influenced the persona of the God of Abraham and that the city of Canaan was one of those unconquered cities still practicing the worship of the female deity. We have only to read the book of Joshua to learn of religious intolerance and the atrocities committed by the Hebrews against the Canaanites at the command of Yahweh.

What this meant for women, as the male deity conquered the female deity may be seen in the difference this made in the law. In Sumer during 2000 BC, a man who raped a woman was put to death. In Assyria, under Indo-European control around 1300 BC, a man who raped a woman had his own wife or daughter raped by the husband or father of the first raped woman. He also may have had the rapist marry his raped daughter. The Hebrews married off the raped daughter to the rapist; however, if she was already married, the raped woman was then put to death. The Assyrian law seems to be the first which prescribes death as the penalty for abortion. Infidelity by the woman was punishable by death at the hand of her husband for both the wife and lover; however, there were no such penalties imposed upon the husband. The change in the law also restricted her economic rights and her rights of inheritance. When the male god deposed the female deity, society changed from a matrilineal to a patrilineal one in the decent of property (Stone). A male deity successfully accomplished both sexual and economic submission of the female to the male. This was done in the name of God and was indeed the first unnamed Crusade. Note that what was done in the name of God had a great deal to do with power and material wealth. This would continue to be the case.

Let us now once again experiment with prayer. Close your eyes now and begin to pray to the Goddess. Women are probably really able to get into this. As they do, they are able to feel validated, powerful and free. Men may not be able to relax enough to pray. Fear may begin to enter the process. Soon, they may feel a need to move their hands to shield their private parts. Praying to a deity of the opposite gender can be frightening! The point is simply this: neither gender of humankind is well served with a deity of the other because it necessitates that the gender, not so enthroned, be rendered powerless. The manifestations of this are both sexual and economic. The way we see God, relative to gender, clearly effects what we see in the world.

As history can certainly teach us, a deity of one gender dangerously becomes the origin of prejudice in the world. If we can justify prejudice in the Source, we can then condone it in the world. The name of God and all that it implies is, most certainly, a matter of great consequence.

As you consider your relationship with the Source of your being, the gender of your deity is an important consideration. As you thoroughly contemplate it, you may decide that some form of change is in order so that you will not continue to add to the body of prejudice in the world. While it is a personal decision, the author believes that until we can begin to contemplate our deity encompassing both genders or, better yet, beyond gender, we shall remain as slaves in Egypt to all of the problems that it brings. Making this leap in faith and understanding gives to each mind and heart the basic elements for the practice of the Golden Rule and thus assists us in removing our barriers to love.

While the reader holds this idea for possible consideration in the back of his/her mind and, as the author continues, she will sometimes intentionally use the term "God" to describe the deity for several reasons. First, this reference to the deity is more familiar in present day culture and, for this reason, it may assist the reader in a better understanding of the ideas presented. It may also help to amplify the problems of gender, perpetrated by such use. From the author's point of view; however, when the word "God" is used throughout this exercise, it refers to a deity of both genders or one beyond gender. Sooner or later, we shall have to change the name of our deity to be congruent with those thoughts.

Contemplate, for a moment, the characteristics of your God. Is your deity a loving God? Then, you probably find it easier to see love in the world and you may find that it is natural to be loving toward others. Do you see a fearful and punishing God? If so, it may be easy to see fearful things everywhere and to experience fear within yourself and to see the need for punishment of self and others. A reaction to this simplistic explanation may be: "I only see what is there." Yes, this is so, you only see what is there for you and you also see from a frame of reference which is uniquely yours. Two people can view the same event and see different things. How one sees God does not exist in a vacuum. It is not separate from the rest of one's life.

As your uniqueness in the world relates to your beliefs about it and to your treatment of others, so does it align with your view of God. For instance, an atheist or an agnostic may easily see hypocrisy among religions and may tend to treat members of a church or synagogue with suspicion and reservation. An individual who sees God as fearful and punishing may see "sin" everywhere and may treat others with a great deal of judgment and scrutiny. One who truly sees God as loving cannot view the world and everyone in it in any other way. Their treatment of others will be loving and kind. The individual who sees God as loving cannot help but be loving and this is the fertile soil which is needed for practicing the Golden Rule. Likewise, it would follow that the reverse is true. A person who does not see God as loving finds it difficult to be loving toward others. This, in itself, would create difficulty in the attempt to treat others as he/she would wish to be treated. The heart of this person wants love but he/she cannot have it because he/she will not give it.

Why is this true? It is true because we seek to emulate our role models. If we can see our God is loving, we shall seek to be loving. After all, God is our Mother-Father Source and we are baby gods. This also transfers to other aspects of life, sometimes, negatively. An abused person often becomes an abuser. An alcoholic often has alcoholic role models. Our role models are extremely important in our conditioning and God is our ultimate role model.

For those who perceive God with fear and punishment, it is easy to skew the Golden Rule into: "Better do to others before they do to you." Such individuals may be afraid that they are not going to get their fair share. To see that they do, they sometimes compromise what they know to be the ethical and fair treatment of others. This enables them to feel guilty, knowing they shall surely be punished. By the way, they are both male and female and they are both homo-and heterosexual.

The fact that we become very much like our perception of God becomes thoroughly evident. In fact, it is woven through the very fabric of our life's experience. There is good news. Because we are responsible for the way our view of God remains, we can change it if it does not serve us well. Yes, we may have acquired the original version of our beliefs about God through our parents and/or our environment, but the evolution of these ideas is totally our responsibility. If changing some of these beliefs better supports our personal relationship with God and the elimination of prejudice in the world, this is exactly what we should do. It is up to us (for every generation has failed before us) to find a way to truly be able to practice the Golden Rule. It is up to us to become the civilization which, not only dreams about this lofty ideal, but finally becomes this ethical principle in action. This *oneness* shall end all separation.

Initially, all of this has little to do with religion, as such, although religion can certainly support it. It has more to do with our deepest, most personal beliefs about God and about how we should treat others. These beliefs can lead us to an acceptable form for their expression. In other words, our beliefs about God may cause us to select a particular faith or religion. As our beliefs change, they quite possibly may lead us to seek another form for their expression or to embrace another faith or religion.

Our God-centered beliefs then become the content and religion becomes the form for their expression. If they are not in harmony, they shall create conflict in our lives. Most people would not do well to believe in a loving God and attend a religious institution where hell, damnation, sin and punishment are embraced. This is because the content and form cannot possibly become synergistic unless there is a framework of congruence. In other words, we seek our beliefs about God and the form for their expression to create combustion within us. This *divine fire* reveals to us our *oneness* with all there is. One cannot be lifted to this higher spiritual evolvement unless both, the content and the form support each other.

So once again, let us go back to the beginning of this relationship. What do you call that Power in the universe greater than yourself? Do you call it God, Goddess, Mother-Father God, Yahweh, Jesus Christ, Allah, Infinite Mind, Brahman or something else? The name itself (except for the problems created by gender) makes little difference for they all refer to the same thing. It only matters that you select or create one that feels right for you.

Once you have decided upon the name, describe this Power to yourself so that you can better understand your view of God. If your God has only one gender, then realize that this may lead you to give that gender preferential treatment. Do you love God or do you fear God? Fearing God may lead you to experience guilt. This may also lead you to punish others, especially those whom you perceive to be different from yourself. Have I said enough?

The way you view God does influence your beliefs which then create your world. What about those who say they do not believe in God nor do they ever think of God? Well, most individuals do recognize that there is something in the universe greater than themselves whether or not they spend much time consciously thinking about it. This is God.

The way you refer to God and the way you perceive God to be yields your beliefs about God which then become the way you operate in the world. This defines how you relate to the Golden Rule. Here is how it works.

God's Name + The Way I See God = My Beliefs About God

My Beliefs About God = My Modus Operandi In The World

My God = My Golden Rule

Cause = Effect

Look at the way you operate in the world and you will know how you view God. If you do not like what you see, you cannot change those effects without first changing the things which are causing them. You are the only person who can make these changes. Others can inspire you toward change but you are the only one who can make change happen in your life.

Change will come about as you define and view your God differently. The nature of that change is entirely up to you as is the way you choose to view your God. If you believe the Golden Rule would truly create a heaven on earth, then you must change yourself, not others, in such a way that you are able to practice it. Use your energy doing your part to make it happen for yourself. Start where you are now. Begin to bring about changes in yourself and you may soon begin to inspire others to change. This is how real change happens in the world, by becoming a role model for someone else.

Experiencing God as anything but love results in barriers to love and to our consistent practice of God's version of the Golden Rule. This version is loving and does not exclude anyone. God's version of the Golden Rule ends judgment and prejudice on earth. Experiencing God as only love removes our barriers to love. Here is how this works.

My Experience of God = My Thoughts / Experience of Life
(Love)   (Love)

Love = My Modus Operandi

Love = My Golden Rule

Love = Love

Once we allow *only* love to be at cause in our lives, we create *only* love in our life's experience. Love can only feel at home in a religious environment that is loving.

The *St. Petersburg Times,* clearly one of the best newspapers in the country, presented an article by Thomma and Cannon (October 30, 1994). They quoted a Gallop and Times Mirror poll to show Americans declining in their confidence of organized religion. It displayed an approval rating of 59 % in 1991 and a 54 % approval rating in 1994. Why, we might ask, does three-fifths of the American population lack confidence in organized religion? Could it be that the perception of the form is too far removed from the content?

Most individuals recognize that the essence of God's message is love. When religious forms which profess to embrace this message do not do so, this displays an ambiguity which naturally translates into disapproval. If an individual feels this way about his/her particular faith or church, would it not be more helpful to find another place of worship where congruence lives, rather than to allow one's disapproval to dispose of the whole idea? Religion can support one's faith in God if it practices what it preaches. It would be well for organized religion to take note of its 54 % approval rating and make whatever changes are necessary to allow itself to ring true to the message from which it draws its inspiration.

Religion emanates from the divine inspiration of one individual. The message then attracts a collection of other individuals open to accepting similar beliefs. Change, therefore, must take place within the individual. The world cannot change until you do. Yes, your relationship with the Source of your being is a very personal matter which effects, both you and your world. You cannot change within, without effecting change in your world.

There is not one gay man or lesbian who does not believe that the world should change in the prejudicial way it treats this oppressed minority. Most everyone would agree that the prejudice which exists for this minority is monumental. This does not make it right. Stemming from false beliefs about God, such prejudice speaks of many people failing to understand the nature of God as love. When judgment, anger, fear and hate become at cause in the world, they can only create more of what they are. This is why gays and lesbians must not hate right back.

Homosexuals and those whom would support them can break this pattern of prejudicial abuse by first realizing the truth about the Power in the universe greater than themselves. Its nature is love, only love and its function is singularly the act of giving. Such knowledge can lead each individual to do their part to bring about change within themselves which will no longer inhibit them from practicing the truth. If gays and lesbians do not lovingly accept themselves, how can the world accept them? If congruence is important to religion, it is every bit as important to homosexuals. What is congruent about hiding one's identity and living "in the closet"?

It does not take a rocket scientist to see that many gays and lesbians live lives of fear and guilt around their homosexuality because of their conditioning. If this were not so, they would not need a "closet" in which to hide. It is time to leave old, unproductive ideas behind. It is time that homosexuals make a commitment to live differently, openly as the beautiful children of God that they are. It is time for all gays and lesbians to realize that, from the very beginning of time, the ideals of humankind have been no different than their own. Living by the Golden Rule cannot be exclusive of homosexuals nor can they exclude themselves from this ideal. They can become a light for the world by kindling the flame of acceptance from within. They can release their fear and disarm the world with love. Their parents and their heterosexual friends can join them in becoming a catalyst for healing prejudice, all forms of it, in the world by practicing the Golden Rule, without exclusion of anyone. It is everyone's privilege and responsibility to perpetuate love, not hate, in the world.

If everyone in the world believed in a loving Power in the universe greater than themselves and viewed this deity as equally encompassing both genders or as devoid of gender, there would be no basis for gender based prejudice. Without this initial form of prejudice, so erroneously attributed to the deity, there would be no sexism in the world.

In a patriarchal society, sexism allows prejudice against women. It also allows homosexual prejudice and every other form of prejudice on earth. The root of the problem is perceiving prejudice in God. Nothing could be further from the truth.

Perceiving the deity as loving and beyond the barriers of gender nullifies sexism in the world. Without this ungodly parent to all forms of prejudice, ungodly expressions of it would not exist in the world. By contemplating God as male we attribute prejudice to the deity. God then becomes the rationale for sexism in the world. If, however, the Supreme Power becomes non-exclusive of gender or beyond gender, then we are able to claim congruence in truly being made in the image of the deity. This is, after all, what we are, both masculine and feminine in our nature. Finding balance of our yin and yang creates lessons for our self acceptance. Embracing our lessons allows us to become more of ourselves. In this scenario, men no longer have difficulty in expressing their sensitive side because there exists no prejudice in doing so and women find no prejudice in expressing their strength and intellect beyond role model barriers.

In a theoretical way, we can contemplate the world as bisexual. If we are capable of loving each other, we are also capable of a sexual expression of that love. Cultural and religious mores inhibit such expression in heterosexuals because it is in keeping with their nature to sexually express with a member of the opposite sex. Bisexuals and homosexuals are not so limited in their sexual expression because it is not congruent with the nature of who they are and who the Source created them to be.

This does not make one form of sexual expression *right* and the other *wrong*. This does not constitute *sin* even though man tries to place this notion in the mind of God. This simply allows for the expression of individual differences based upon the individual's own deity-created nature. When man attributed gender preference to God, it became the origin of and the poetic license for all forms of prejudice in the world. Likewise, the elimination of gender prejudice in God, while also viewing the Power as a loving deity, will eliminate prejudice in the world. It will take not one, but most of us, thinking these thoughts and standing up for them in the world. That the Source of our being is only love and beyond all limitations of gender will truly change the world.

REFLECTIONS

Mother-Father Source of my being, help me to see You beyond the limitations of gender and to light my flame by replacing every thought I ever had of You with only love. Love is what You are and, being created in Your image, love is what I am.

I am willing to express my true nature of love in the world through everything I say and do. I am willing to value love and to be loving in all my relationships, both personal and professional. I am willing to remove my barriers to love.

Mother-Father Source of my being, You have forever inspired humankind with the same standard of behavior. Let me not fail myself by failing to learn Your most important lesson as I lay down all forms of prejudice. Help me to lift others by lifting myself higher as I become a congruent example of love's expression in the world.

As I think, so I do. As I do, so I become. I commit myself to love and to the expression of it through applying the Golden Rule in my life. May I always treat others as I would be treated.

CHAPTER FIVE

Reinventing The Source

We have seen the difficulties which are inherently present in the old, patriarchal view of God, as well as in the older matriarchal view of the Goddess. Because each is exclusive of the other, both create separation from the Source and from each other. This separation then becomes a license for prejudice which first appears as sexism in the world. The ungodly gender becomes less valued than the Godly gender and this creates inequities for the ungodly gender. The placing of value on one thing over another gives rise to further separation and to elitism. In this context, the individual says: "This is better than that. Male is better than female. Heterosexuality is better than homosexuality. White is better than black, etc." This allows for a situation where "better than" becomes the preferred nomenclature to "different from". The individual then allows him/herself to look down upon the ones whom are not "better than".

The basic difference in the two descriptive positions is that "better than" has value attached to it and "different from" does not. As "value" interjects itself in relation to the human condition, prejudice evolves which allows us to separate from each other. Such a separation is precluded by a separation from the Source. From a perceived gender separation in the deity, all other forms of prejudice can be born. Even an unconscious awareness of gender prejudice in the Source can give to mankind poetic license for the other forms of prejudice. "If God has prejudice, so can I."

As women have become less valued in patriarchal society through the patriarchal "One God" religions, history clearly communicates that it has led to her sexual and economic servitude to the Godly gender, the more powerful and more knowledgeable male. Cultural and religious conditioning has convinced society that men emerge from the womb automatically knowing how to handle money better than women do and women emerge from the womb without even the capability to decide what is best for her own body. Such are some of the myths of patriarchy.

Society has continued to see evidence of such beliefs through centuries of economic dominance, rape, violence, domestic abuse and especially in the current battle over abortion rights for women. As long as men continue to fight for the right to control a woman's body, there are patriarchal ownership issues on the agenda. They would not otherwise dare to do so. Would they tell their neighbor what to do with his/her property? Such a directive would not become an appropriate activity without an ownership prerogative. Let's get real on this issue. Is there not something wrong with the picture of men fighting for the rights of the unborn offspring while perpetuating and condoning violence upon the female giver of life? Men have asserted their *divine right* (their ownership rights) to control a woman's body through their brotherhood with a male God. On the other hand, women have found that man's patriarchal God has been lacking in love and fair treatment in relation to the female gender. Such would assume gender prejudice in God which can be understood as a perception of God in *our* own image.

Ever since the God of Abraham dethroned the Goddess and devised a plan for her continued subjugation through the story of Adam and Eve (a male version of Paradise), woman has been separated from the love of a patriarchal God and dominated by His extensions in the male gender by *divine right*. According to Merlin Stone, the Levite priests used the Adam and Eve myth to suppress the female religion. This faith had developed over thousands of years and it was rich in symbolism. Serpents and sacred fruit trees were common symbols of this religion. The serpent was an established symbol of the Goddess. It was, after all, the problem of woman listening to Her which led to the expulsion of humankind from the original state of bliss called the Garden of Eden.

In the Near and Middle East, the serpent seems to have been primarily revered as female and associated with wisdom and prophetic counsel rather than known as a phallic symbol associated with sexuality. The Goddess Nidaba, the first patron deity of writing, was sometimes depicted as a serpent. In the Sumarian town of Dir, the Goddess was referred to as the Divine Serpent Lady. The Goddess as Ninlil, revered for bringing the gift of agriculture and civilization, was believed to have the tail of a serpent. The Goddess was also called Great Mother Serpent of Heaven. She was described as the Divine Mother who reveals the laws, a Serpent Goddess and an interpreter of dreams of the unrevealed future (Stone). This enables us to better understand the patriarchal religions' position on divinatory matters through methods of the occult such as astrology and the psychic sciences. We must not forget the extension and the outcome of this position when many women were wrongfully burned at the stake in the name of God.

This position was a repudiation of the female deity although we know that Moses was quite comfortable using divinitory powers of the unrevealed future as well as the symbol of Her (the serpent) in his display of God's power with the Egyptian king. Since Egypt was a place of Goddess worship, this story also has connotations of a power struggle between the male and female deities. We know that Moses and his patriarchal God eventually won.

According to Stone, sculptures found in Sumer, dating to around 4000 BC, portray the female figure with the head of a snake. There clearly was a linking of the reverence for womanhood, giver of life, magic, prophetic wisdom, interpreter of dreams and revealer of the laws with the symbolism of the snake. Whether or not Freud would be appalled at this idea, examining the Bible and its references to snakes from this perspective could certainly be an enlightening experience.

In Babylon, the Goddess as Ishtar was also associated with the planet Venus. She was also known as She who Directs the Oracles. The widespread association of the serpent with the female deity was, most likely, the reason such symbolism was used (*to her detriment*) in the Indo-European myths and in the story of Adam and Eve (Stone).

On the island of Crete, the snake appears more often than in any other Mediterranean area, portraying, through the unearthed artifacts, the Goddess and/or her priestesses holding snakes or having them curved around their bodies. This reveals their integral part in religious rituals. This evidence of the Serpent Lady as Goddess dates back to 3000 BC and was probably brought there by the Egyptians, where even the picture of a cobra was the hieroglyphic sign for the word Goddess (Stone). The cobra was known as the Eye, the symbol of mystic insight and wisdom and it was worn upon the foreheads of other deities and Egyptian royalty. We are also able to correlate this symbol with *Enlightenment* in the esoteric and mystical view as is depicted by the snake curling around the chakras, opening and activating their full potential, as it makes its ascent upward to the Eye, often referred to as the Third Eye, on the middle of the forehead. This Eye is also associated with the pineal gland. Activating and opening this chakra is associated with intuitive and prophetic vision as the snake progresses onward through the seventh chakra achieving or activating *Enlightenment* in the individual. The great mystics of all religions speak of this process.

The Eye was later known in Egypt as Hathor and Maat. The Goddess as Hathor, whose name means House of Hor, was also associated with the male deity Horus (Stone). It is interesting to the author that the female deity, those who worshipped her as temple priestesses and those of her gender would later be known by a name sounding very much like its derivative. As Stone relates, a preserved text recounts a story that Hathor had been the serpent who existed before anything else had been created. She then made the heavens and earth and all that existed upon it. In this story, she was angry for reasons which are not clear. In her anger, she threatened to destroy all of creation and to resume again her original form of a serpent.

In Greece, the Goddess at Delphi proffered divine revelations which were spoken by the priestesses who served her. Pythia was the name of the woman who brought forth the oracles of divine wisdom. Coiled about her tripod stool was a snake known as a Python. The earliest accounts considered Python to be female. In later Greek writings, the Python would be considered male. Greek legend tells us of the priests of the male God, Apollo, taking over the earliest of the female shrines and of the murder of Python by Apollo (Stone).

The Philistines are linked to the worship of the Serpent Goddess of Crete and the female deity revered in Canaan. The Philistines, known as arch rivals of the Hebrews in the Old Testament, are believed to have come from Caphtor (believed to be Crete), which the Egyptians called Keftiu. The migrations of the Philistines to Canaan are placed around 1200 BC. in the time of Abraham. The Philistines settled primarily in the southwest portion of Canaan which came to be known as Philistia, the origin of the name Palestine. Along with the Philistines came the religion of the Serpent Goddess (Stone).

The Hebrew tribes would later make their exodus from Egypt and the Bible would record that, during this period in the desert, Moses came to possess the "brazen serpent." A bronze serpent would be found hundreds of years later in a shrine in Jerusalem which would be destroyed as a "pagan abomination" by the Hebrew reformer, Hezekiah because of its association with the Goddess religion (Stone).

It is no accident that, in the story of Adam and Eve, we have a serpent poised as the spoiler of Paradise. This serpent is the symbol of the female deity and She is held totally responsible for the *fall*, working her magic through a dimwitted woman whom had no identity apart from man and his rib. When such a myth was developed, accepted, perpetuated and preserved in the Bible through the authority of the Levite priests, society would experience a major reinvention of the Source. History documents this reinvention as well as the trials and tribulations of God's appearance as male.

While the details of the deity's prior journey as female are not as prolific for us to examine, we can assume that such a reign was not totally fair and equitable to the male gender. We can also see that their frustration, sexually and economically, could very well have led to Her dethronement. We clearly went from one extreme to another, seeking a balance through the deity which could not be found through the extreme nature of either position.

Slowly, we are coming to this realization as men and women begin to learn to trust each other. We can see the embryonic beginnings of this taking place in the 20th century as women moved into some positions of power, evidencing excellent work without the castration of their male counterparts. We can also see some basic beginnings of women taking back the control of their own bodies. Men, especially religious men in the Fundamentalist mold, still seem unable to abandon old ways of thinking which still display their ownership prerogative in the name of God. As they allow love to grow in their hearts, it will surely displace the issues of control and fear. They shall then willingly relinquish all old or new ideas which do not treat others (all others) as they would be treated. As men find the heart and will to do so, they will also see that their lack of control does not mean abandonment by the female gender, nor need it lead to their own control by them. It is time for such a healing to take place.

A cleansing of world consciousness is at hand as humankind again struggles to reinvent the Source. As the last vestiges of male violence, aggression and their aftermath plays themselves out in the name of God, a new deity consciousness emerges like a Phoenix from the ashes of the old and extreme ways we have chosen to envision the Source of our being. This cleansing shall constitute a gender-balanced reinvention of the Source and this shall become the cornerstone of the *New Millennium*.

This reinvention of the Source will be quite different from the previous two. It shall be an equal combination of them and therefore, a balanced rendition of gender in the deity which then goes far beyond gender to righteous acceptance of all of the Source's creations. This morality can be *only* loving and giving to all people. Having this form of deity realization and role model acceptance, we cannot continue to maintain our irrational ideas, our judgments and our prejudices. There is no separation from the Source nor from each other. This is how we shall remove our barriers to love.

In such a world, can anyone practice anything but the Golden Rule? This author thinks not because the projection of our thoughts into the world becomes reality. This is life's creative process. As we dismantle the barriers to love in our own perception of God, we change our role model in a significant way which positively effects our actions in the world. If the Source is only love, then so are we. Such a role model will serve to elevate our thinking and our actions.

Reinventing the Source in a manner which is non-exclusive of gender eliminates the origin of prejudice in the world through elimination of sexism in the deity. If the deity does not sanction such behavior, neither can we. If we no longer discriminate based upon sex, we shall become more willing not to condone other forms of prejudice in the world. This will help us to realize our connectedness with each other. As we do so, power no longer need be used to dominate others. No longer shall we take pride in imitating the animal kingdom. Power can then be used as a privilege for communication and communion with our Source, that we may learn more of what it means to be loving and giving. As we truly learn these lessons, we shall delight in taking action upon them. We may then become better practitioners of the ethical treatment of everyone in the world, regardless of their differences from us because we shall not feel separated from each other.

As we begin to shift our use of power from control of other people and situations to communication with our Source, what kind of tools are we going to need in our toolbox? We shall but need to use tools which have been there all along, the tools of meditation and prayer; however, for the first time, we shall feel compelled to use these female and male forms of deity communication in a more balanced manner.

To reflect upon our unbalanced implementation of prayer and meditation so far, we shall begin by examining some of their definitions. Beginning with *The American Heritage Dictionary*, New College Edition, the first two definitions of prayer are as follows: "1. A reverent petition made to a deity or other object of worship. 2. The act of making such a petition." Prayer is talking to God/Goddess and usually asking for something (petitioning). It is active, an attempt to control the situation, more masculine in its approach and it evolves through the conscious mind. Meditation is defined as "a devotional exercise of contemplation." It is better understood as listening to Goddess/God. It is passive, intuitive, feminine and is an activity more associated with the subconscious mind. Bringing together these aspects of ourselves in peace and harmony on earth is the desire of the soul. Perceiving the Source through only half of the truth stands as an obstacle to this fulfillment. It is the marriage of the masculine and feminine principles within us that we seek. A balance here achieves the peace we seek in the world but find within ourselves.

As we try to make sense of the history of both matriarchal and patriarchal religions from the practice of prayer and meditation, we can see the lack of balance in each, with the Goddess worshippers perhaps being more concerned with the intuitive, listening process and worshippers of the patriarchal "One God" religions (Jewish, Christian and Muslim) being more concerned with prayer, as a process which speaks to God to the exclusion of sufficient listening to Him. In a traditional worship service of the patriarchal religions, prayer is generally more common than meditation. It is usually very specific, often repetitive (a standard part of the worship) and directed by the male rabbi, priest or minister of a male God. This one-sided communication with God becomes the model for our communication with each other and becomes the cultural standard for the same imbalance between the sexes. Whenever one person speaks, to the exclusion of listening to the other, communication breaks down.. We see this evidenced through the breakdown of marriages and relationships.

It is also interesting to note some differences between the patriarchal "One God" religions and the religions of the East where there is more than one deity and where all of them are not considered to be male. We find that meditation assumes a much more important part in the practice of religions which evolved in India, China and Japan. Where female deities are a part of the religious form, the intuitive aspect of listening to the Source assumes a greater importance. We see this played out in our culture as well where women tend to be better listeners than their male counterparts and men tend to be more dogmatic and directive than females. There are, of course, exceptions to this; however, these may be viewed as cultural generalities.

It would seem that the patriarchal religions place more emphasis on talking to and petitioning God than they do on listening to Him while the matriarchal religions place the major emphasis on listening and relating through the intuitive to the female deity. This also plays out in the culture, with women being considered more sensitive and intuitive than men. We could also say that each position is off balance by ignoring the strength of the other. On a mundane level, each position seeks what it has momentarily forgotten but knows to be true at a superconscious level, that each of us has both a masculine and a feminine side of our nature. Finding balance within is our heart's desire. Each individual, whether male or female, heterosexual or homosexual, is seeking balance within of his/her own male and female characteristics.

We clearly see the imbalance of this situation in contemporary society as men struggle with their sensitivity and women with their assertiveness. Homosexuals also struggle toward balance of the masculine and feminine aspects of their nature. This is what the individual struggle is all about and it is unfortunate that the concept of "value" in the human condition creates discrimination in this balancing process. The cultural belief is that one struggle is "better than" the other, that the heterosexual struggle is "better than" rather than "different from" the homosexual one is a belief which keeps all of us in Egypt. Another important detriment is our attachment to being "right". It is no mistake that anger has always created itself in the instant we are wrong and determined to be right.

While many of us realize the fact of such imbalances in our attempt to find balance within ourselves, we often act as if we are mystified from where these problems come. As long as our perception of God is mirroring this imbalance, we are destined to remain in our ignorance and error. Let us not forget that we cannot change effect without first changing cause (referred to here as our perception of it).

Our thoughts create our world. There is no other way for life to create. The lifeblood of our thoughts cannot create other than itself. A horse does not create a dog. It creates another horse which is like itself. In the very same way, hostility in the world is created by hostile thoughts. We are destined to create that which we are in our minds and hearts and these creations are what we experience in the world. "If I do not like what I see, shame on me!"

Relative to our quest of seeking balance in the masculine and feminine aspects of our nature (whose symbols can be understood through the activities of prayer and meditation), a gendered or an unbalanced approach can only bring more of itself. As women get stuck within the framework of not being able to ask for what they want and men get stuck in the framework of being unwilling to listen, imbalance continues to perpetuate itself in the world. Likewise it is, that a preacher who kills an abortion doctor has hateful thoughts. Let us realize, once and for all, that the end never has justified the means. The end and the means are one and they are created by a thought. We always know the nature of thought by the thing that it creates.

The way out of this box demands that we analytically look at the problem so that we might creatively resolve it and balance can be found. Centuries of failure might lead us to preclude that we have not yet done so. Cause is continuing to create effect and our thoughts of love are clearly not at cause in our mundane world. If they were, they would create *only* love. This would bring peace, which is another name for balance of the masculine and feminine energies within us. We can further conclude that if we are not at peace, we are out of balance. How we got there is what our minds and hearts must understand so that our souls might progress. If we are out of balance, our thoughts must also be, for they are creating our life experience.

Why is our culture and society patriarchal anyway? Is it not because our view of God is male? After centuries of trying on the many manifestations and evolution of the patriarchal God of Abraham, we find Him to be just as lopsided and unacceptable as was the female deity by the name of the Goddess. It is time for us to allow their union to occur within our minds and hearts. We must perceive balance in the deity, before we are able to experience it in ourselves. It is when we balance our thoughts of gender in the Source that we can find balance within ourselves. Only then are we capable of balancing issues of gender in the world.

Living in this reality, no longer will one gender be persecuted for any reason. No longer will one gender be more powerful than the other. No longer will one seek to dominate the other. When we remove gender prejudice from our view of the deity, we shall be able to remove it from the world. Because it appears to be the origin of all other forms of prejudice, removing it removes the foundation for other forms of prejudice in the world. If our view of the deity is devoid of prejudice, we shall not consider ourselves entitled to have prejudice. *Divine right,* becomes reserved for the divine. Only love for all others becomes our *divine right* from a deity without prejudice, as love creates love in the world. Without enmity and judgment in our thoughts, there can be no prejudice in the world.

Does this mean that women, homosexuals, blacks, Jews, Muslims, disabled people and any other group whom have experienced prejudice in the past, will retaliate for the injustices of the past? It simply could not be when love is at cause in the world, for it can only create more of itself. In such a world, "different from" replaces "better than" and standards of behavior are judged by their adherence to the Golden Rule.

With a balanced view of the Source of our being and in a balanced world, we shall seek and find a balance of the masculine and feminine aspects of our nature. This has always been at the very core of the lesson to be learned from life. Some will learn this lesson best as male and others as female. Some will learn it best as homosexual and others as heterosexual. Some will have the best opportunity of learning this as a member of one particular race or through a body with a particular set of challenges. Who are we to question the judgment of anyone's soul and their Source? All of this is little more than window dressing anyway with the real issue being the goal of balancing the masculine and feminine principle within each one of us. For too long now, we have been so adversely affected by our prejudice of the form that we have totally ignored the content of the message. This is our lesson. Eliminating prejudice from our deity helps to eliminate prejudice in us and finding balance in the Source helps to create balance within us. This is how the earth shall heal as a loving world removes its barriers to love.

This reinvention of the Source has already begun, the climax of which shall be felt at the end of this century. Some of its requirements have already begun to manifest through political laws of the land such as the abolishment of slavery, women's right to vote, civil rights legislation, non-tolerance of anti-Semitism and various human rights initiatives which include protection for those with disabilities. It is interesting to note that the only prejudiced group, still with no uniform protection in the law, are homosexuals. It is clear that this is the most extreme form of prejudice that exists.

One of the first steps in fighting prejudice is through protection by the laws of the land. This must be done to allow society, as a whole, to break its bad habits of the past. It can be compared to the stitches in an incision. They are needed to hold the flesh together until the wound can heal. Gay rights are not unnecessary. They are mandatory if prejudice against homosexuals would end. As the fair-minded, ethical and altruistic elements of society realize this and understand that homosexuals are the only group not so protected by the laws of the land, they shall demand better of their politicians, and politicians shall demand better of themselves. Every group and every individual deserves to be protected from prejudice. This includes a woman's right to make choices regarding her own body without church or state intervention in the same manner that men make choices about their own bodies.

We are at a precarious moment in time when the religious right would mask the separation of church and state to prejudice both women and homosexuals in the name of God. This must be seen for what it is: ungodly and unchristian. These ideas speak of separation from the Source and attempt to perpetuate separation in the world.

The final times of this new reinvention of the Source are at hand. This is the challenge of the new Millennium. As we allow the male God of the sky within us to marry the female Goddess of the earth, love can reign for a thousand years. The moment of responsible choice also is at hand and it is up to us to decide whether or not we desire to participate in this new world. If we allow this *divine marriage* to take place within us, we must eliminate prejudice in the deity and in ourselves. This permits us to become an usher for the *New Age of Love and Peace* on earth.

Those who will not abandon their spiritual pride and their attachment to being "right", even when their self-righteous beliefs and methods have failed so terribly to express love, shall be carried away as the earth purges and cleanses itself. The cataclysmic events of ending an age with barriers to love may combine natural disasters with the last remaining vestiges of aggression and prejudice to bring a time of love and peace for everyone.

Those who would choose not to participate may find themselves in the wrong place at the right time. Those who would serve humankind in the *New Age* shall be guided from within by the balance of the Source within them. Anyone can choose to join this worthy mission of love and peace by joining with minds and hearts whom would reinvent the Source, devoid at last of prejudice and filled with *only* love. These brave souls shall end the separation from the Source because they cannot do otherwise as they achieve the balance which they seek within themselves.

A deity of one gender can no longer make sense to unifiers of the Source for they realize this is what they have been seeking through thousands of years of lessons left unlearned. A male *or* female deity is equally unacceptable if prejudice would end on earth. Only balance of the two will do, both within the Source and within the self.

This transition into a *New Age of Love and Peace* can be accomplished right now by individuals with willingness to remove their barriers to love. This is all it takes to eliminate personal prejudice in all of its manifestations. Humankind must first remove it from their perception of God before they can remove it from themselves. This noble work can be done with or without the help of religion. If religion desires to be a part of the change at hand, it must change all aspects of its beliefs which are sexist and prejudicial and promptly put them into practice. It must reveal its creative thoughts through its actions in the world. It, too, must welcome the *divine marriage* within itself and must live totally and congruently from that space. Anything less than this will be unacceptable to those whom would unify the Source within themselves.

Source unifiers are able to see the Truth and are unaccepting of ambiguous messages. Those religions and faiths which cannot lovingly assist in Source unification and would instead support separation from the Source through the division of gender preference and the extension of any form of prejudice, shall be swept away in the churning of the earth as life is cleansed and love prepares to reign on earth. This is the time for the Golden Rule in action.

Established religions can and should take the lead in this movement although it certainly is their prerogative not to do so. They cannot lead, however, without first purging and cleansing themselves of prejudice. While this is possible, it will be difficult for many religions that have had a long time to perpetuate bad habits of exclusion and prejudicial elitism. Some of the newer, non-denominational faiths may find it easier to effect the changes needed for leadership in the *New Age of Love and Peace*.

If established religions do not take the leadership role by eliminating prejudice within themselves, new religions will be created. It is the nature of the human condition to choose to experience the religious content of the deity through an appropriate form, but humanity shall demand that the form be *totally* congruent with the message. Source unifiers realize that their experience of the past, without such congruency, led to hypocrisy in the world and thus, to a turning away from the Source. Source unifiers are not willing to go down that road again.

A new concept of the Source of our being must begin with a name which is non-exclusive of either gender. The names, God and Goddess, are equally unacceptable because each prejudices the opposite gender and this gives rise to barriers to love. "He" and "She" are not suitable pronouns for referring to the Source. This new concept of the Source of our being establishes the Source as *only* love. It manifests on earth through our loving treatment of all others and becomes the Golden Rule in action.

This new concept of the Source is not heavily burdened with theology nor does it require an interpreter to understand the Source. The things each individual is capable of understanding about the Source, at any particular time, are revealed directly to each Source unifier. It becomes as important to listen to the Source as it is to express oneself to the Source. Gone is the need to petition the Source for things of the material world. Source unifiers are in touch with their own power to create what they desire through synergistic thought and action. Their greatest desire is for more knowledge of the Source which they continue to receive from within.

Source unifiers are at peace within themselves and their peaceful thoughts create peace in the world. They are at peace with the elements of earth, air, water and fire. They treat the air, the earth and its' bodies of water with the respect, love and gratitude implied in the Golden Rule, as they celebrate the *divine fire* within themselves. They realize their interconnectedness with all things. All is *One* and *One* is all.

At last, Source unifiers find balance of the masculine and feminine principles within themselves. Anger and aggression are no longer out of control and grown men are free to weep and to listen. Assertiveness is balanced and lovingly accomplished to the incredulity of women. Every member of the human race learns that giving is receiving, as our spiritual nature finds its realization in our consciousness and we choose to live from this awareness. Source unifiers find *The Way* as they make their joyous, final journey *Home*.

REFLECTIONS

Mother-Father Source of my being, help me to reinvent You in all the ways in which I would reinvent myself. Help me to find Your perfect balance within myself. I am committed to being a Source unifier. No longer am I content to be a guest at Your wedding feast. I open my mind and heart to welcome the Divine Marriage of the masculine and feminine in me as I find it in You. It brings to me a balance and a peace which passes all understanding.

When I have it in me, I can give it. When I give it to all others, the extension of it strengthens it in me through synergy. I am free; I am free at last. I am the Golden Rule in action. I am, finally, One with You and One with everyone in the world. I have traded separation for love and I have found freedom in my world.

Help me, Source of my being, to help others to find their balance within as they also reinvent You within their minds and hearts in ways which remove their barriers to love. Help all of us to cleanse, through water and through fire, the thoughts which allow each one of us to create with only love and to express it in the world.

CHAPTER SIX

There Is Only Love And Fear

Have you ever thought that absolutely everything that we experience and express in the world is primarily processed through an inner core of either love or fear? If a life experience inwardly rebounds against an inner core of fear, our reaction to the experience will be fearful and anxious. If the experience rebounds from an inner core of love, our response will be loving and peaceful. We may view this as a continuum on which all of life's experiences may be placed. The nature of the response serves to create what we perceive as reality while it strengthens the inner core of love or fear within us. In other words, love creates more love and fear creates more fear, both in ourselves and in the world.

It is important to realize that the life experience itself is not creating the love or fear. The response of either emotion, or any degree in between their extremes, is facilitated by the inner core of the individual against which the life experience rebounds. The nature of the inner core then influences our response and thus creates more of itself. An example will enable these ideas to make more sense.

Dora goes to work one morning and is told by her employer that business is slow. Overhead expenses are much to high for the revenues currently being generated and therefore, her position must be eliminated. Her performance has been good and she will surely be missed. The employer is willing to give her a letter of reference and handles the situation as gently as possible under the circumstances.

Dora's response will clearly demonstrate if she is coming from an interior core of love or one of fear. If it is based in fear, she can only give birth to fearful responses such as these: "What am I going to do? Suppose I cannot find a job? How am I going to pay my bills? This cannot be happening to me!" These fearful responses will create physiological counterparts in her body known as stress. If allowed to persist for periods of time, unresolved and unrelieved, they could lead to physical problems or disease.

From this we can further extrapolate that fear throws us off balance, creates anxiety and causes the body to break down. When we respond in fear, it strengthens that inner core of fear within us, enabling us to more easily resonate, amplify and expand it. It permits us to experience it more thoroughly in succeeding occurrences in the future, as life continues to imitate what is inside of us. It is actually causing it although this is usually more difficult to see. This follows the principle of like attracts like. If we are fearful inside, we shall attract many fearful experiences in the world.

Granted, this is not the way most people think about life. They tend to give far too much weight to the particular life experience itself as the creator of the response. The question to be answered is who is in the driver's seat? Is the individual a billiard ball or a cue ball in the game of pool that we call life? If they claim to be a billiard ball, they are able to embrace a victim consciousness. This allows them to place too little emphasis on the inner core of the individual as the determinant of the response. This also speaks of personal responsibility. How much or how little are they willing to accept?

It is a fact that if the inner core is love, the response must be loving and peaceful and if the core is fear, a fearful and anxious response will usually emanate from it. From this perspective, it is of paramount importance that we get in touch with the nature of our inner core. As long as we deny its ability to be at cause in our lives, we shall blame others. More importantly, it will disturb our inner peace.

We have seen Dora respond from a core of fear. An inner core of love would produce a far different response. She would probably be thinking and saying things such as this: "I understand your position and I appreciate your willingness to recommend me to other potential employers. Since this door has closed, I know that an even better one will be opened for me. The Source of my being has always taken care of me before and I know that my needs are being met now even if I am not consciously aware of it and that I am being led to something better." Such a response would be healthier and more self supportive. It would enable Dora to experience peace instead of anxiety. Such a response would allow her to flow with the river of change in life rather than resisting it, for all change is ultimately good.

The choice is always ours to make. We can respond to any situation in life through love or fear; however, the choice for love becomes more difficult to make when the inner core has fear-dominance. It does not make the choice for love impossible. It only makes it more difficult. Desire for change and belief that positive change is possible is often all we need to move through this difficulty.

If we recall the story of the little boy who wanted a pony so badly that he was willing to dig through a dung heap to find it, his desire and belief was: "With all that horse puckey, there must be a pony in there somewhere."

No matter how things appear, there is good to be found in every situation, especially if desire and belief are a part of the scenario. An attitude of: "There's a pony in there somewhere", also maintains balance within us which reduces anxiety and, instead of allowing stress to harm the physical body, we can actually strengthen it. Such a response will further strengthen our inner core of love, thus enabling us to rebound with more of it in the future as we respond to other life experiences. A loving response also helps us work out the problem more expeditiously. Free from anxiety, we can think better, organize our job search with a more focused intent, better present ourselves at the interview and bring the matter to a fruitful conclusion.

The reader may be wondering: "Isn't this just positive thinking?" Yes, in a way it is but it is far more. It is the power source behind positive thinking. It is, indeed, what makes positive thinking possible. It is an inner core of love. Without it, no amount of dreaming or desire will make a positive thinker. Have you not heard an individual say: "I try to think positively about this but I just cannot do it." They are right and what we are discussing here is why they feel they cannot do it. Their inner core on this particular issue has fear-dominance. As long as it remains so, it is easier for them to respond with fear which often takes the form of negative thinking. It then creates a negative outcome and reinforces more fear within the inner core, and round and round it goes.

It is useless to tell someone to think positively unless they are willing to acknowledge that an inner core of love is possible and they value it enough to make what for them is a difficult choice. Until they do so, they simply cannot think positively. Try with all their might, they shall fail until they are willing to change their inner core from fear to one of love-dominance. Negative thinking is born of fear. It retreats and says, "I can't". Positive thinking is based in love. It advances and says, "I can".

Most individuals are endowed with varying degrees of both cores. There is the inner core of love which functions on certain issues and a core of fear which comes into play on others. The size and extent of each core's domain is the indicator of how successful and fulfilling the life is. The greater fear becomes, the greater the tendency one has to retreat from the Source of our being and the world. The greater love becomes, the greater is one's tendency to integrate with the Source and the world, to contribute to it and to help the world to heal. The former is restrictive and gravitates toward a little white coat with the pulled down sleeves. The latter is expansive and gravitates toward healing and freedom.

While these beliefs are applicable to everyone, they are particularly applicable to women and to the homosexual community. Women might ask: "How does cultural conditioning affect my self worth and my achievement in the world: How fear-dominant is my inner core?" Homosexuals might ask:

"Does a life in the "closet" indicate anxiety or peace? Does a lack of self or world acceptance emanate from an inner core of fear or one of love?"

Every other prejudiced group can ask similar questions. Are they experiencing life from an inner core of love or fear? There is generally a high degree of fear to be found in individuals or groups of individuals whom are prejudiced in the world. In examining a holy book source on love, we find a Pharisee asking Jesus a question which he answered thusly:

> Master, which is the greatest commandment in the law?
>
> Jesus said unto him, Thou shalt love the Lord thy God with all thy heart, and with all thy soul, and with all thy mind.
>
> This is the first and great commandment.
>
> And the second is like unto it, Thou shalt love thy neighbour as thyself.
>
> On these two commandments hang all the law and the prophets.
>
> Matthew 22: 36-40

There clearly is no recommendation here for fear. Concluding that the Source of our being is love and that we are too (if we will only allow ourselves to rise to our potential) can free our inner core from fear. We are here to rise to this potential by doing our own work. Accepting total responsibility for our lives becomes the road that takes us home to what we are. Love is truly what we are; fear is but a block in our remembrance.

When we encounter a life experience, how we think about it and how we behave tells us the nature of our inner core related to this particular aspect of our life. It is made of either love or fear. If our thoughts are fearful, they shall elicit fearful behavior and such thoughts shall make us feel anxious. This is a clear indicator that the inner core is fear. When our thoughts and behavior in response to a life experience are peaceful and devoid of fear, we know that the inner core to which they relate is love. On such issues, we cannot fool ourselves.

There is no contest as to which we would prefer so how, we might ask, do we change this inner core of fear to love? How do we step off a moving train? The author knows of only one way to accomplish this. Through the process of forgiveness, we can change a core of fear to love. Before the reader says, "Oh yeah, I have already done that", contemplate for a moment this example. In Matthew 6: 12, we have been told to: "Forgive us our debts as we forgive our debtors". Suppose this were interpreted to mean: "Cancel what we owe others in direct proportion to our willingness to cancel what we think others owe us."

Under such circumstances would we not become more willing to stop blaming others and more willing to cancel our unforgiving thoughts of self and others? The author believes that we would certainly be more inclined to try. To become willing to forgive is the first step. To forgive is to cancel the effect upon ourselves of unpleasant things of the past. It has nothing to do with forgetting that these things happened. It has to do with changing the effect they continue to have upon us.

If we look at some of the examples of Jesus and forgiveness, as evidenced through the Gospels, we find there are several references which may be interesting to the reader to pursue. His very life seems to have been a format for forgiveness through the canceling of effect. In Matthew 9: 2-8, we have Jesus forgiving the paralyzed man who was lowered on a stretcher. Here Jesus clearly canceled the effects of whatever was going on within this man to create and maintain the paralysis. In John 8: 3-11, Jesus forgives the woman who was caught in adultery. His words and actions clearly canceled the effects of her action for those whom would have stoned her. His ultimate act of forgiveness was for those who crucified him (Luke 23: 34). In doing so, he was not condoning what they did but said, essentially, "This has no effect upon me." He was canceling effect as he operated from an inner core of love.

When one considers that Jesus was a Jew who was trained in the Jewish tradition where there may have been a stronger inclination to fear rather than to love God, we can see that he was faced with the difficult decision of choosing to respond with love and not with fear. In making the more difficult choice, he therefore canceled its effect upon himself and upon the world. He became the ultimate example of operating from an inner core of love.

If we compare this example with the many antithetical examples (done in his name), we are able to see the painful truth. Those thoughts and actions which are often portrayed as "Godly" and "Christian" and which evoke fear are, in fact or in truth, neither Godly, nor or Christian. They emanate from man's own inner core of fear. Into this picture frame we can place all of the prejudice in the world. Where there is prejudice, there is always fear. We can also say that for prejudice to end in the world, fear must be conquered.

Prejudice can only continue as long as people allow thoughts and ideas to evoke fear within them. This is only possible as long as an inner core of fear predominates within the prejudiced individual. In other words, one fears the thing about which one is prejudiced. (We are already in touch with the fact that, such prejudice springs from an irrational thought). To illustrate, we shall "try on" a few ideas which may illuminate this fact. "If I allow her to be too independent, she will not need me. If she does not need me, she may leave me."

Such thoughts have led to the perpetuation of prejudice against women. It makes no difference that the thoughts may be irrational from the start. She just may not leave because she loves you; but if you do not love yourself, you cannot believe it. Fear restricts you from doing so. Guilt about the way you have treated her in the past may also be present. The extent of your inner core of fear whispers to you what you must do about it should she step over your accepted bounds of independence. Depending upon the degree of your inner core of fear on this issue, you may be given to pouting, shouting, spousal abuse or death.

Aching within the violent heart is often a desperate need to be loved and to avoid being abandoned. This does not make the violence acceptable. It speaks, however, of futility, for that love cannot be found outside the self until it is present within. When this is so, love is found everywhere. The high incidence of domestic violence speaks of a world "looking for love in all the wrong places", or better stated, through all the wrong methods.

It is this very process of forgiveness, or canceling the effects of the past for ourselves, which breaks down the core of fear within us and rebuilds it with love. As we continue with this process, we amplify the core of love within us. This is the real purpose of forgiveness, to change the way the past continues to effect us. We shall learn more about this and more of how to accomplish it in the next chapter. As the various aspects of our core (relating to the different aspects of our lives) progressively change from fear to love, we experience more love within us through a larger core of love and it attracts more of itself in our world. Love can only rebound love as we give and receive that which we are in the world. This is why we are here and this is how we play our part in creating heaven here on earth.

Since the mind can only focus on one thing at a time, perhaps homosexuals should stop worrying about the world and what others think about them. The world shall heal when there is enough love within it to do so. Would it not be more fruitful for everyone to employ their energies upon themselves to heal the fear within their inner core?

As we do our own personal healing, we become an example which can help the world to heal. A wonderful tool for this healing process is available through the *Course In Miracles*. Using it daily will help those individuals who are interested in eliminating fear in their lives and allowing love to grow. There are also many other spiritual tools which could be helpful. The point is that choosing a spiritual tool helps to make the process easier than trying to go it alone.

The choice is up to you. Which would you prefer, love or fear? Which feels better? Which allows you to grow and to become all that you can be? In choosing love, you must form a definition of forgiveness which allows you to embrace it and apply it in your life. As the *Course In Miracles* says:

> "It is your forgiveness that will bring the world of darkness to the light. It is your forgiveness that lets you recognize the light in which you see. Forgiveness is the demonstration that you are the light of the world. Through your forgiveness does the truth about yourself return to your memory. Therefore, in your forgiveness lies your salvation."

An example which deserves examination for the prejudiced homosexual population is: "If I allow the world to know who I am, they shall reject me." Such a thought is born of pure, unadulterated fear. Yes, this fear may very well stem from centuries of conditioning and evidence of maltreatment but homosexuals must realize it is this very thought that they think which keeps them enslaved. To escape, they must cancel the effect this fear has upon them. This can only be done by risking the rejection through becoming known as homosexual in those areas of life which are emotionally charged by fear. It is what is called "coming out of the closet".

It is not important that such a proclamation be made on prime time television but that every homosexual search his/her own heart for areas where becoming known as a homosexual evokes personal fear. These are the areas where risk taking has the potential to eliminate fear and to increase their inner core of love. Each homosexual person may be at a slightly different place on the "coming out" continuum. One person may say: "I do not care if my personal friends know about me, but my parents just could not handle it". Another person may say: "Everyone else can know about my nature, just do not tell my father"! A very public individual may say: "My friends and family may know about my orientation but public acknowledgment will ruin my career".

The point is this: wherever the individual has fear associated with acknowledgment of who they are, that is precisely the area where they would most benefit from taking the risk. Making the difficult decision builds the inner core of love in relation to self. When homosexuals love themselves, they will not be afraid to be known for who they are. When this happens, then the rest of the world can heal its irrational fears and prejudice with regard to homosexuality.

Let us go back to the premise of like attracts like in the universe and revisit this through an example to see how this works. This will allow us to see how thoughts create themselves in the world. While the example speaks of homosexuality, every other prejudiced group could use their most prevalent fear and create a similar example for themselves.

LIKE ATTRACTS LIKE

<u>Thought</u>		<u>Actions</u>
"If I allow the world to know who I am, they shall reject me."	=	**Perpetuation of Fear**
"	=	**Don't Ask; Don't Tell**
"	=	**Rejection of Laws Granting Equal Rights for Homosexuals**

It seems clear that homosexuals must begin to accept responsibility for the world which their fears have created. Through the canceling process of forgiveness, they shall accomplish this goal. As they change the effect this fearful and causative thought has upon themselves, they shall change its effect in the world.

We can use a more mundane example to further illustrate this idea. Let us imagine the example of a frightened, cowering dog. Let us further assume that this dog has been beaten and maltreated by many. What, we might ask, has the ability to heal its fearful condition but love? If this dog could allow a gentle, loving person to diminish its fear by petting it gently, soon it could allow itself to become more loving and trusting. While this would generate more love flowing between both parties, this moment cannot come to pass unless the dog makes the difficult decision to risk fear for love and acceptance. It is a canceling process of forgiveness which paves the way to love. In taking the risk, the dog cancels the effect which the past maltreatment has upon it from that moment on. In the very same way, all prejudiced groups can free themselves of fear.

To risk fear for love implies that past judgments must be set aside. It matters not that these may be the very judgments of others which the prejudiced group has allowed to precipitate their own internal fears. This is always difficult for the prejudiced group because they usually feel foolish. Somehow, they bought a bill of goods which allowed fear to rear its ugly head within them and they must now cancel its effect. While this idea is not always easy to own, it is required if further progress is to ensue.

For instance, women have believed the judgments of males in authority. These judgments have been that women are not as intelligent, that they are the property of men, that they are dependent upon men because they cannot make it on their own, that the place of women is in the home and that they must tolerate any form of treatment rendered to them by their male master. This equates to her father, husband/boyfriend and even to God, Himself. Such are the cultural judgments about women, at least, since the God of Abraham. These ideas would not have gained power in the world had women not been convinced to believe them.

It is not the intent of this book to explore the many reasons why women decided to take the bait of belief regarding judgments which prejudiced them. An entire book might be written on this subject. We can, however, recognize that fear precipitated all of the reasons on that list. Women must move through those historical fears to diffuse the emotional power of the many judgments about them which have been born of irrational thoughts. This will enable them to reject the negative judgments they have accepted about themselves. Judgment has been a powerful oppressor of women.

Homosexuals also need not look very far to see the effects of judgment in their world. In fact, judgment against homosexuality may be one of the most profound vehicles for judgment on planet earth. Does this make homosexuality wrong? Of course not; this is the way the Creator has created some individuals to be. Does it make judgment about them acceptable? Certainly not, for judgment leads to prejudice. So, judgments against homosexuals lead them to also be judgmental as like attracts like. "If everyone is judging us, why should we not judge them right back?" While this is an understandable response, it is Neanderthal in its understanding. It cannot find its way to peace and love as the history of humankind so clearly substantiates.

By judging in return, homosexuals direct the cycle of abuse to perpetuate itself and, more specifically, to return to them. The *Spiritual Law* reference for the judgment implication of the Golden Rule was succinctly delivered by Jesus in his Sermon on the Mount when he said:

> Judge not that ye be not judged. For with what
> judgment ye judge, ye shall be judged; and
> with what measure ye mete, it shall be measured
> to you again.   Matthew 7: 1-2

A timeless example of this is the Holy War which continues to be fought in the Middle East.

Heterosexuals and homosexuals should be especially mindful of practicing judgment against each other if they would be free from its effects in their lives. Everyone should also be cognizant of where judgment begins. Judgment begins in thought. This should be especially apparent to homosexuals since so many of them continue to live "in the closet". Most are not retaliating in deed, for they are staying hidden, but they continue to retaliate in thought and this creates their world. As long as homosexuals continue to judge others by standards of fear, hate and anger, they shall continue to support this cycle of abuse in their own lives. Like women, many homosexuals have also taken the bait of belief regarding the judgmental thoughts others hold about them. They must diffuse and dismantle these judgments to find wholeness in their lives.

This may be a level of responsibility which many homosexuals are unable to accept upon their exposure to such thoughts for it is always easier to blame others. This is understandable but the questions they might ask themselves are these: "Has my fear, hate and anger regarding these terrible things others say and do in response to my nature brought me anything of value? Has my negative response to such words or actions changed things for the better for myself or for my brothers and sisters? Have my thoughts and reactions created more tolerance in the world?" The author asserts that they have not. Prejudice and judgment against homosexuality still abound.

Even those times when judgmental thoughts have led homosexuals to the retaliating actions of fighting back, as was the case with Stonewall, they have not brought about necessary and sufficient change. In fact, the only redeeming factor in such behavior may well have been to acknowledge and accept themselves for who they are and, at least for those brief moments, "to come out of the closet". In such instances, fighting back became the negative aspect of the positive ideal of self acceptance.

Perhaps homosexuals can agree that what they have done has not worked too well. It has not worked because change begins from the inside out and as long as homosexuals are judgmental against those who judge them, they shall continue to condone and perpetuate judgmental abuse in their lives. If they could see that such individuals are acting from fear born of irrational thought, they might draw a different conclusion. What is needed is education which emanates from a loving space.

Homosexuals have instead projected the problem to be the other person's problem. As long as it is contemplated in this light, it is easy to become judgmental. Suppose they were to turn that around and accept it as their own problem and correct the judgment problem within themselves? They could not then project it toward others. As they offer no fuel for the fire, the fire must go out. It is their judgment thoughts about themselves and others which have fed the flame of judgment in their world. Becoming responsible for their own part of the judgment problem will serve as a spiritually correct example for rest of the world that it may heal.

Judgment then, is a habit pattern homosexuals must break if they would end the cycle of prejudicial abuse against themselves. It begins with their thoughts about themselves. "If there is not some part of me that believes I am a bad person, I cannot become fearful of you or angry with you when you call me a bad person. If I am not angry with you, I cannot think punishing thoughts about you, nor can I do or say punishing things." Let us think about these thoughts for a moment in terms of Matthew 7: 1-5.

> Judge not, that ye be not judged.
> For with what judgment ye judge, ye shall be
> judged: and with what measure ye mete, it shall
> be measured to you again.
> And why beholdest thou the mote that is in thy
> brother's eye, but considerest not the beam that is
> in thine own eye?
> Or how wilt thou say to thy brother, Let me pull
> out the mote out of thine eye; and, behold, a beam
> is in thine own eye?
> Thou hypocrite, first cast out the beam out of
> thine own eye; and then shalt thou see clearly to
> cast out the mote out of thy brother's eye.

To allow this passage to illuminate emotionally charged judgments against homosexuality held by some heterosexuals, let us understand that sexuality is part of human expression. A part of everyone's quest in life is to balance the feminine and masculine principle within themselves. Some are given to do so as homosexual and some as heterosexual. This has more to do with the soul and the Creator's business than it does with the cultural mores of humankind.

Those at the far ends of the feminine-masculine continuum seem to be the most judgmentally vocal against homosexuality. Males at the masculine end of this continuum and females at the feminine end of the same continuum tend to be the most judgmental against homosexuals, and more specifically, of their own particular gender. Macho males tend to hate male homosexuals and ultra feminine females just cannot understand what lesbians do. Males and females, at both ends of the continuum, being more imbalanced within their own masculine and feminine energies, seem more able to hold sexual bias. It is this imbalance which then becomes the "beam in their own eye", and such imbalance easily leads to judgment and prejudiced actions in the world. While sexual bias is only one form of judgment, there are many, many other judgments which are held.

We tend to think of judgment as action while failing to be aware that it begins as thought and that our thoughts create our world. Since the thoughts we have had have not created a better world, should we not be bold enough to change them? The place to begin is with ourselves by becoming aware of how judgmental we really are. We can begin to get in touch with this if we will take the time to write down every judgmental thought we have in one period of 24 hours. To follow through on this, we might carry a piece of paper titled JUDGMENTS for 24 hours and write down every judgmental thought that occurs in that period of time.

If we are willing to confront ourselves on judgment, it is important to be totally honest and thorough in writing down every single judgmental thought we have about everyone and every subject. No one need see this but us and we do this for one purpose alone, that is to get in touch with the manifestation and form of judgment within ourselves.

If you are really brave, take these judgments back to the Prejudice model presented in Chapter 1 and work backwards to uncover the irrational thought(s) causing them, and then forward to undo the negative action(s) which are keeping you in "Egypt" (bondage). This will help facilitate your healing process.

This exercise leads us to discover that the judgments which we hold within ourselves are really about ourselves. Everything we think we see outside is actually inside us. The world is but an echo chamber for the music playing within us and all of life is created from within. If there is judgment within us, we shall experience it in our world. Could this be the real meaning of Matthew 7: 1-5?

If we accept this meaning, what implications does this have for women, homosexuals or for any other prejudiced group? We can only conclude that since there is so much adverse judgment in the world against these groups, their own interior landscape must be churning with self judgment and lack of self love and acceptance. Otherwise, homosexuals would not have created a "closet" in which to hide, and prejudicial remarks or actions directed toward any prejudiced group would not be capable of evoking a negative response. If prejudiced groups were truly at peace with who they are, nothing and no one could disturb that peace within them. They would not take the bait. Judgment then, would not beget judgment and the cycle of abuse would end.

So, how do we dissolve these judgments once we get in touch with them? We shall learn more about that in Chapter 7 when we discuss the subject of forgiveness. For now, it is enough for us to begin to understand that the judgments we experience from the world are not unrelated to the judgments which we hold about ourselves. This does not make the world right for the same *Spiritual Laws* apply to everyone and we all have need of healing our tendency to judge.   The areas of individual judgment experienced and expressed, are but markers on the path of life which indicate the areas which are not yet whole.

With this in mind, can we begin to look at judgment against all others in a different light? Can we begin to relate to it through personal responsibility instead of universal blame? Can we begin to see it as a call for love? If so, then we can truly change the world. As the *Course In Miracles* says:

> "Judgment and love are opposites. From one
> Come all the sorrows of the world. But from
> The other comes the peace of God Himself"
> (*the Source, Itself*).

If you would like to know more about the *Course In Miracles*, please see the reference section of this book.

REFLECTIONS

Mother-Father Source of my being, help me to see that all of life rebounds against my inner core of love or fear and this is what I see. I desire to see and experience more of love in the world and I am willing to heal myself to do so. I have no time for blame; I have no time for judgment. I have only time and energy for my own personal healing to which I now dedicate myself. Until this is accomplished, I cannot bring positive change to the world.

I have a commitment to love, to becoming it, to expressing it, to receiving it. Help me, Mother-Father Source of my being, to open myself to a new understanding of forgiveness which enables me to practice it. Thank you Mother-Father Source, for Your assistance with this bold step of personal responsibility as I find my way upon the path of personal healing to end prejudice in myself and in the world.

Help me to put aside judgment of others by healing those things within myself which wrongly echo in the world as I refine the transmission of my thoughts. By decoding and dissolving the negative thoughts I have about myself, I become able to love myself as You love me.

I am willing to look at the judgments I have held about myself with the knowledge that this is what has created my world. I am willing to change my world through personal responsibility. Universal blame has not worked in the past and I now willingly set it aside to reclaim my power and to create a better world. As I break the cycle of judgment in my life, I create less judgment in the world and I help everyone to heal. Thank You for the blessing of becoming a catalyst for healing in myself and in the world.

CHAPTER SEVEN

Forgive, Forgive And Forgive

Forgiveness is the releasing of ideas which are based in fear. When we do so, we create more room for love. Because love feels better than fear, forgiveness is necessary for happiness and wholeness. Forgiveness then, is a canceling process for the fear which we experience.

At some level of our being, each of us knows the importance of forgiveness, yet on any given day when the subject is broached, typical responses might be as follows. "Oh God, not this again! I am tired of hearing this is what I need to do. I know that it is important (I really think that it is impossible) or I have already forgiven everyone and I am ready to go on with my life." Wrong!

Forgiveness is not a thing you do once and then conclude that it is done forever, but rather, a process through which you live, applying it to your daily life. You are not finished with forgiveness as long as you have past memories accompanied by negative emotion or as long as painful and upsetting things are happening in your life. It seems safe to conclude that forgiveness may be applied forever. If it is to become part of our daily business, it is important that we learn to view it correctly so that we can fully embrace the support it offers us.

One of the most common and erroneous beliefs to dispel about forgiveness is that it is doing someone else a favor. Forgiveness is not letting someone else off the hook but refusing to allow yourself to remain on the hook any longer. To forgive is to realize an error was made and become willing to release it, so as to cancel its effect upon yourself. The part of the error which is affecting you now was made in your mind. This is why you must release it. Forgiveness is essentially self-serving and necessary to you for living a healthy and happy life.

Each one of us is desirous of healing ourselves and forgiveness is the key to doing so because it helps us to remove our barriers to love. No matter how bad things seem, a part of us wants to be loving toward others and we wish to receive loving thoughts and actions from others. When we are able to accomplish this, it truly feels wonderful. So, why does this not happen all of the time? The answer seems illusive because it is often hidden below our conscious awareness; however, the mechanics of it are truly simple. Think of your mind as a computer and your life as a reflection of the programs running it. The original program was perfect love but we have altered that program because of the times in our past when we experienced less than perfect love. Because of these experiences, we made erroneous assumptions that our program was inaccurate and we changed it by adding some programs based in fear instead of love. This can also be described as living by our will instead of by the Creator's will.

The parts of the program that we have changed to less than love can only bring a less-than-love experience. This is the way that computer programs work. The world has also referred to this idea as: like attracts like. It really cannot do otherwise. This means that we shall experience exactly what we are. The parts of our program which we have changed to less than love are destined to bring results which are based in fear. Our task then becomes one of seeking out those parts of our program which are creating a less-than-love experience in our lives and purging them to return the program to its original state of perfect love. This enables us to experience the Source of our being in the world through our own spark of divinity. "The Mother-Father Creator and I are one."

We desire to make these changes because less-than-love experiences do not feel good. Fear is painful and unnecessary even if we are responsible for having changed our program in the way that has produced it. The good news is that we can again alter the program to produce another effect. Since there is only love and fear, a lack-of-love experience must be based in fear.

It is important that we make this recognition without being too hard on ourselves. If we did not have some flaws in our program, we would not need to be here. If we were not in need of personal healing, we would not need to use the practice of forgiveness.

Because we are human, sometimes we miss the mark. We sometimes give out less than love and this is what the world calls "sin". In this context, we define sin as an error response because it is devoid of love. In fact, this is the only way that we sin, by giving out less than love, for when we do, we treat others as we would not wish to be treated. When this happens, we have merely made a mistake which can be corrected and canceled through forgiveness, a tool to be applied daily for the purpose of achieving and maintaining wholeness.

The process of living and the results of our life's experience give us the data for our evaluation. This data is comprised of thought, emotion and action. If the thought or emotion is not based in love and/or the action is not loving, there is a correction which is needed in our program. If we do not make the correction, it will continue to bring the same results. The question to be asked is: "Do I like the results I am getting?" If not, we must work to correct the situation. This correction will usually involve the healing of memories in our past through forgiveness and this will bring a greater restoration of ourselves to love. As we expand the amount of love in our program, we enable ourselves to express and experience more love in our world.

In reviewing our data of thought, emotion and action, we come face to face with our dynamic interactions with others. They are either loving or they are not. The less-than-loving interactions are caused by our program flaws, and pain is the signal which helps us to identify them. Until we do so, we cannot change the program. Once we identify and release them or cancel them out through forgiveness, we have the opportunity to avoid the same painful results in the future. All of the people in our lives and all of our interactions with them are vitally important in helping us to identify the parts of our program which need to be changed. Our relationships then provide us with the necessary feedback to magnify our program flaws. Pain allows us to see them. We will not be inclined to change the flaw until we can see it. Everyone knows that seeing is believing. The world describes this as the scientific method of proof. This is what is valued in the material world.

Our evaluative data is found in our relationships with others. We have parental, professional and personal relationships and they are either loving or they are not. Where they are lacking in love, they are painful. Pain either becomes the catalyst for change or it creates more pain. If the needed change is made, the cycle of pain is interrupted and love is restored. Forgiveness then, becomes the tool and the process by which we restore ourselves to love.

To examine how this works, we shall look at two individuals. Living and loving together usually provides a multiplicity of situations for interaction and for differing points of view. One example might be the different ways they tend to keep house. For purposes of illustration, we shall use an example of a same sex couple whom we shall call Jim and Bob. If this should cause the reader problems, consider going back to Chapter 1 to work with the four step Prejudice model to deal with your feelings so that you can work your way back to the irrational thought(s) which are causing your response before continuing with this chapter.

The choice is forever present for us to cancel irrational thoughts if we choose. By doing so, we more easily neutralize fear, emotion and judgment. Without judgment, there is no prejudice in us. Without prejudice, we can begin to treat others as we would be treated.

As we continue with our example of a male same sex couple (any other couple could be substituted), we find that Bob never puts anything away and Jim is a compulsive neatnik. When Jim comes home and finds Bob's jacket on the chair in the dining room, dirty dishes in the kitchen, the bathroom a mess and Bob out by the pool taking a sun bath, Jim hits the ceiling and an argument ensues. As Jim accuses Bob of being an inconsiderate slob, Bob reacts in anger. Jim's reaction is less than loving and so is Bob's. Both reactions therefore are based in fear and both result in pain.

Let us now look at this situation more closely. What was it that upset Jim? Was it really a jacket hanging on a chair? That, indeed, would be a very powerful jacket. What about the dirty dishes in the kitchen? Can dirty dishes really cause such turmoil? What about the messy bathroom? Can inanimate objects out of place create anger? No, of course not. When we contemplate these things devoid of emotion, we are able to see the truth. It is not any of these things in themselves which create the problem. It is our thoughts about these things which bring us pain.

From where do these thoughts come? They come from our memories of the past. There is something in Jim's memories of the past which is causing his reaction to this situation in the present. Maybe this was the way Jim's father acted when things were out of place and maybe this is how Jim was treated when he did not put away his things. Maybe his mother was a slob and never kept an orderly home and Jim was embarrassed by her. Maybe there is some other reason. Only Jim knows and this information may not necessarily be in his conscious awareness at this moment. If Jim could only identify and cancel it, he would be able to experience this situation differently. This is what the forgiveness process does. Its purpose is to enable one to see things differently. Even though Jim's preference might never be to experience a messy home, his reaction to it need not create negative emotion within him and he need not respond in a manner devoid of love. Because he has done so, this tells him there is something to forgive, something to cancel from the past because it is adversely affecting him now. He is in pain.

He will tend to repeat this situation and to experience his negative reactions over and over again until the part of him which needs to heal gets his full attention and he heals the past memories which are affecting him now. Suppose there was a time in the past when he was severely whipped because he did not put away his toys as a child? As he forgives himself and his parent, he can then change the effect this situation has upon him in the future. Then, when he encounters things out of place, he may not have to go ballistic.

We shall later discuss a method for accomplishing such healing but what about Bob? Jim is certainly not alone in this negative emotional response. Bob experiences Jim's response to the situation of his messiness as devoid of love. He allows Jim to become the cue ball which becomes responsible for his reaction. Bob then reacts in an angry, disempowered manner which is also less than loving.

This is what the author calls the cue ball philosophy. While the reader will recognize it as expression which is basically reactive, it is explained in greater detail in another book by this author entitled: *The Homophobic Healer.*

This book also has additional work on forgiveness which may be helpful to the reader. Other work which may be extremely helpful in the category of forgiveness is the work of Dr. Michael Ryce through his workshop available on audio and video cassette, "*Why Is This Happening To Me Again?*" and the books and tapes of Dr. Gerald Jampolsky may also be helpful. The author cites their work as references for this chapter and highly recommends that the reader pursue their inspired messages. Both men also happen to be students of the *Course In Miracles*, as is the author. All sources mentioned are recommended to the reader for further amplification on the subject of forgiveness.

Because this forgiveness chapter is the most important chapter in this book, it is also recommended that the reader continue to reread it and work with the concept of forgiveness until there is an understanding of it which can be applied to his/her experiences in life. If one does not understand forgiveness in such a way that one can practice it, one cannot bring positive change into one's life.

Bob is not angry for the reason he thinks. In this moment, he is unaware that Jim is really responding to memories in his past which need to be canceled or deleted through forgiveness and not to Bob himself who is merely triggering these memories. If Bob could only be mindful during Jim's outburst that this is not about him (it is really about Jim and memories of his past which need healing), then Bob could have a different experience of Jim's reaction. He may not like Jim's reaction, but experiencing it differently would enable Bob to respond without also withholding love. So, one reason Bob becomes angry is because he perceives Jim's response to be all about him and not about Jim, himself.

This is not all Jim's problem. Another reason why Bob responds angrily to Jim's outburst is because Bob has his own memories of the past which are also in need of healing and the stimulus of this present experience is triggering them. Perhaps Bob's mother was an alcoholic who ranted and raved at Bob when she was drunk? When she did so, he felt unloved and unsure of what he might have done to deserve the outburst. She also may not have been a good role model for Bob in the area of housekeeping skills. Perhaps his father had abandoned them because of her drinking. Bob also has his own forgiveness agenda which is needed. What is happening at the present moment did not begin now but is based in past memories.

Because the memory needs healing, it is trying to get Bob's attention. Until it does and Bob heals this memory through forgiveness, this situation will come up again, again and again. It will also create similar negative emotions when it does come up and these will build in intensity with repetition. This will allow Bob to feel unloved every time someone yells at him. This too, can be canceled through forgiveness, which brings a new level of understanding. Such will eliminate fear and restore love to himself. By so doing, Bob is able to respond in a loving way. He still may not like the response that Jim is having but he is able to respond to it in a manner which does not withhold love because he can become aware that it is Jim's problem.

All we ever truly want from others is for them to respond to us in a loving manner and that is exactly what they want from us. Our heart's desire is to be capable of living by the Golden Rule. So why is this not always our experience? The reason for this is that all of us have memories of the past which are in need of healing. Until we heal them through forgiveness, they will cause us to withhold love.

Whenever we withhold love, we experience pain. Emotional (or physical) pain is how we know there is at least one memory of the past which is in need of being healed. Pain is our alerting signal and our wise conclusion is: "When I am in pain, the error causing it lies within me. I am the only one responsible for my thoughts and I am responsible for my behavior." We are not usually consciously aware of how cause is creating effect. Jim thinks that Bob is the cause of his reaction. When we are not in touch with the real cause, it is easy to interpret the effect as the cause. Bob thinks Jim's outburst is the cause of his (Bob's) feeling unloved and unappreciated. We are seldom upset for the reason we think.

Jim sees Bob's behavior as the cause of his distress and Bob sees Jim's reaction as the cause of his anger. Wrongly diagnosing the problem keeps them from taking proper corrective action. This permits the problem to persist. Any couple will readily admit that the problems which come up in their relationship usually seem to happen again, again and again. This, in itself, should point to the fact that they are not getting to the root of the problem. It is the placing of blame outside of self which precludes them from finding the answer. They shall never find it looking in the wrong place. While no one can control what the another person does, everyone is responsible for his/her own reactions.

As long as Jim sees Bob's behavior as the cause of his distress, Jim will not try to heal anything in himself. As far as he can see, it is not his fault. It is Bob's fault. Placing blame allows him to continue to experience the same distress. This will continue to repeat itself over and over again. Even if this prompts Jim to leave the relationship, the same situation will continue to happen with others. It will happen because Jim is trying to place the blame for his distress outside himself. Nothing can change until he realizes that the cause of his distress lies within himself and he begins to search in the right file for the information at cause in this situation. Until he recognizes it in himself, he cannot cancel it. Forgiveness is the tool which enables him to do so. Jim can then find a way to deal with the situation without withholding love. The same holds true for Bob. As long as both recognize: "When I am in pain, the error is mine, not yours", the tendency will be to assume responsibility for it instead of placing blame upon the other person.

By learning how to avoid withholding love from as many situations as possible, we progressively and surely return to our perfect and natural state of love. Until we do, we find ourselves seeking out pacifiers which do not ultimately work. Money and things of the material world are excellent examples of this; not that it is wrong to have them but that they cannot be adequate substitutes for love. This caused Peggy Lee to write a song called "Is That All There Is?" There is great wisdom in this song. While it is always commendable that one would seek to find the answer, it cannot be found unless we look in the right file.

Let our emphasis then be upon cleansing and removing everything from our being which causes us to withhold love. The canceling process of forgiveness then becomes the tool and the process through which to live our lives on a daily basis for the purpose of returning to what we are. Returning to our original program of perfect love, we affirmatively acknowledge our connection with all things and move toward oneness with the Source of our being and with each other. This is the purpose of the life experience.

Forgiveness has important implications for all prejudiced groups. With so much prejudice against them, it is easy for them to get stuck in blaming others. They must avoid doing so, for this will only cause them to withhold love out of fear. Every response which is fear based is an unhealthy one which ultimately brings pain. This is not the response anyone would seek in return, so they must not set up and perpetuate the framework to receive it.

Let us pursue, for a moment, the meaning of "Give and you shall receive". If one gives out love, this is what one receives; if one gives out less than love, one gives out fear. In doing so, one nurtures oneself to become more fearful. "Give and you shall receive" did not mean give any old thing and you will receive exactly what you want. It also did not mean that you will receive exactly what you gave. It meant that you will receive exactly *AS YOU HAVE GIVEN!* Did you give out of love or fear? If you gave out of fear and you are the one who is experiencing it, it must be your fear, right? All that you experience is always about you and all of your experience is created by the programs stored in the computer of your mind. Your past is continuing to create your present. Alter your memory of it and you create a different experience. This is what is accomplished through the canceling process of forgiveness.

In the beginning, the Creator perfectly programmed your computer with love, so, what happened? Well, there were some momentary power surges and failures which caused you to drop memory. Some of these surges and failures were caused by the energies of traumatic events of the past. Somehow you stored some of them as memory and they merged and became part of your program. The elimination of some of your perfect love memory and the addition of trauma and inaccurate data stored as memory has now become the program under which you are functioning. You have mixed light with dark, apples with oranges; no wonder there are glitches. You had a perfectly good program to start with but because it was modified with error, it has created error in the results and in your perception of them. You are seeing "as through a glass darkly" yet the results look real. How do you find your way to the truth?

Ask yourself the question: "Do I feel pain when I contemplate the results which look real?" If the answer is "yes", then the way to the truth will be found through the use of forgiveness. It will help you find the error in your program. The error and its correction will involve the healing of one or more memories of the past. Forgiveness is not the doing of a favor to someone which is wrongly deserved. It is the process of undoing our own erroneous thinking by finding error in our program, drawing different conclusions and storing them as part of the program.

Why bother? Well, first of all, it will feel better to experience love instead of fear. It will allow you to become more of what you can be and you will help the world to heal. You can only influence positive change through the example of that which you are. If for no other reason, some of the error in your program just may be a virus calculated and programmed to self-destruct the entire operation at a certain period in time. Need I say more? Since forgiveness is the tool and the process for correction in the information age, let us now begin to explore how to use it.

Forgiveness may be viewed as a five step process to be used on a daily basis whenever you experience pain as negative emotion. We earlier used the example of the situation between Jim and Bob. You might use any situation or subject familiar to you which causes you pain and/or a negative emotional response such as anger. With paper and pen, take yourself through the five step process which follows. Use it often to take personal responsibility for all that you think and feel. Use it to heal your memories of the past so that you can live more fully in the present. Make a commitment to use this process daily for 21 days and then evaluate the results for yourself.

FORGIVENESS

A Process for Releasing Fear, Anger and Guilt
and Restoring Love

I.   THE SITUATION: Describe the situation which causes you pain, how it makes you feel and what your feelings make you want to do about it. This particular person or subject and/or this situation causes me to feel _______ and it makes me want to do ______.   "When I replay this situation in my mind, do I feel love?" If not, forgiveness is necessary

II.   THE CAUSE (Assigning Responsibility): Where does the cause of this lie? As I reflect upon this, I know that I am responsible for what I feel. When I am in pain, I am the one who is in error. If I want to punish, I am feeling fearful, angry or guilty. I am then unable to feel love. By restoring love, I displace fear, anger and/or guilt. Nothing is happening "out there", it is all happening inside of me. I am responsible for everything I see, feel and think. I am seeing you and/or this situation now through my feelings of fear, anger and/or guilt or I would not be upset. You and/or this situation are triggering my pain but you are not the cause of my pain.

III.   THE ROOT OF THE CAUSE: Lies in my memories of the past through the program that was stored in my subconscious mind when some inaccurate data of fear was added to my original program of perfect love. I shall now momentarily suspend my fear, anger and/or guilt regarding this event and, with eyes closed, I shall allow my emotion to form a gigantic magnifying glass which enables me to see more clearly. I recall when I felt I was accused of a similar situation by____________ and/or when and/or how I was similarly punished by _______________. This part of my past was experienced in fear, anger and/or guilt. These memories of the past have created this situation in the present. I can change the situation by recognizing the past as the program for the present and I can change the situation by changing the program and by choosing to experience love instead of fear, anger and guilt.

IV. THE TRUTH: What I really wanted from you was to bring this up for me, so I could heal my memories of the past. I now release them to the Mother Father Source of my being and restore myself to love. I give thanks to the Source of my being and to you for helping me to heal memories of the past and to change my program for the better in the future.

V.   THE RELEASE AND RECONSTRUCTION: I am willing to release my fear, anger and/or guilt because they do not feel good. Until I do so, I am not able to experience love. I am willing to forgive myself for the error I made in associating you with a situation of the past. I now own the real cause of my pain which I willingly release. I forgive those in my past for failing to experience and express love to me instead of fear; and I forgive myself for wrongly using this experience to alter my own program of perfect love. I send all of you and myself a message of peace and love. By experiencing love, I reconnect with the Source of my being. In doing so, I reconstruct with love as I allow it to restore itself to me. I release all negative emotion surrounding this issue. I am empowered and good things are possible for me. I am at peace and all is well.

This forgiveness instrument was inspired through the work of Dr. Michael Ryce. See references for more complete information on the availability of his work.

Working with this process will help you to get in touch with things of your past which have been hidden from you and which are influencing you now in ways you never before realized. Getting in touch with these new realizations will help you to heal. As you do so, you will find yourself expressing and experiencing more love in your world.

At the moment of your inwardly personal revelations, you may experience an emotional response. Allow yourself to experience it fully. If you feel like crying, do so. It will help you to release the pent up energy this issue has bottled up within you. Afterwards, you may feel sad, melancholy or depressed. Do not fret about this. It is but regret for years of wasted energy wrongly used and it will pass. Things sometimes get worse before they get better. It is all a part of the healing process.

Make a commitment to use the five step process on all people and situations of your past which cause you pain whenever you contemplate them. The things you will discover about yourself will absolutely amaze you. Then, on a day to day basis, as things come up to anger or irritate you, sit down and do a five step forgiveness process on them to continue learning more about yourself. Correct as many faulty programs as possible. As the process helps you to produce more love through your thoughts, emotions and actions, life will become more of itself. You will love the life you live as you find yourself progressively returning to your natural state of perfect love.

Prejudiced groups and individuals may be quick to say: "What about them? Are they not the cause of my pain?" The author would assert that *they* can only amplify the pain which is already there within you. If you remove the fear from your core, there is only love. When there is only love, even prejudiced thoughts and actions of others cannot disturb your peace. When your peace cannot be disturbed, there is no energy to fuel prejudice in your world. This is why you must forgive yourself before the world can be forgiven by you. Forgiveness is the path that takes you home to what you are.

REFLECTIONS

Mother-Father Source of my being, help me to cleanse my life of fear and find the way home to my natural state of perfect love. Help me to see forgiveness in a different light. Help me to see forgiveness as the tool of freedom, the pick and shovel that works so well to free me from the past and heal my unproductive memories.

I am committed to positive change in my life. I shall use the five step process daily for 21 days, working on my past and on day-to-day happenings in my life which cause me pain. I shall then evaluate the way I feel. If I like the way I feel, I shall continue this work forever. Thank you for Your help with this evaluation.

Mother-Father Source, help me to accept more love in my heart and to become an example of more love in the world. Bless my parents for loving me the best way that they could. Bless every person in my life for providing me the opportunity to learn more about myself and to heal. I send out to the world my message of peace and love as I move forward upon the path that takes me home to my natural state of perfect love. I accept this now as my life's goal and the most important thing I can do to help end prejudice in the world.

CHAPTER EIGHT

Love Is What You Are

As you progress through the canceling process of forgiveness, you return to what you are. Love is what you are. While you are focused on fear, it precludes you from knowing your true self. The more fear you remove from your life, the more energy there is to experience your nature as love.

You have a certain amount of energy and it is your choice as to how you use it. If you spend 90 % on fear, there is only 10 % left for love. As you use the canceling process of forgiveness, you begin converting your fear percentage to love and as your inner core achieves a love dominance, life becomes an easier process. Upsetting things still happen but they seem to occur less frequently and when they do, you are able to deal with them in a manner which becomes a blessing to all.

As your inner core of love expands, you experience less anxiety and more peace. It is interesting to note that the purpose of the most widely prescribed drugs in the 90s are used for the purpose of lessening anxiety and creating a more peaceful state. Tranquilizers and anti-anxiety drugs provide a physical solution to a spiritual problem. Prescription drugs, illegal drugs and alcohol are used to change anxiety into peace; however, their effects are only temporary and sometimes, even damaging. We have the microcosm of physical reality intending to effect the macrocosm of spirituality. What we have not done spiritually, we are attempting to do physically. We are waging the same battle on all levels of being as anxiety battles peace and fear battles love. By refusing to resist, we can allow peace and love to win. They flow naturally with the river of life unless we try to swim up stream.

Fear creates anxiety, and by pushing through fear comes understanding and release. The canceling process of forgiveness allows peace and love to win. Yogis and Zen Buddhists have long used less injurious methods than prescription drugs, illegal drugs and alcohol for allowing the experience of peace and love to be present in their lives. This is the object of our heart's desire and the goal which we are seeking.

We look for peace and love in drugs, alcohol, work, recognition, sex, relationships and material possessions. We seek and we seek but we never find them there because we are looking in the wrong place. They cannot be found outside us. By seeking inside, we can find the peace and love which has been there all along, waiting for our recognition and remembrance. We are able to mine the gold we have been seeking by going inside ourselves to use the tools of forgiveness, meditation and prayer. Everything "out there" then reflects against this brilliance and we are able to see its reflection in the world. This is the only way we can find peace and love in the world, by allowing it to mirror back to us that which we are. Our world simply cannot be what we are not. By experiencing peace and love within ourselves, we are then able to experience them in the world.

This means something important and very specific to all prejudiced groups who see the world attacking them. Your world can only do as you do and can only be as you are. It is more than interesting that within the prejudiced group of women, there is the militant feminist at one extreme and the peaceful, prejudiced female at the other extreme. Both are unhappy with the gender prejudice which they experience, but one extreme seems to exhibits more pain than does the other in relation to the same prejudice.

Among homosexuals, there is the militant activist at one extreme and the peaceful, prejudiced (and often closeted) homosexual on the other. Likewise here, one extreme seems to exhibit more pain than the other. The same is true among blacks and every other prejudiced group. There are the attacking and the peaceful extremes of every prejudiced group and one extreme appears to be in greater pain than the other. One might further postulate that it is the painful end of both extremes which brings about change. This is not exactly true. While they may sound the gong of recognition in the world that indeed, a problem does exist, they cannot be the solution to the problem in their attacking state nor is the problem usually solved without them.

These reflections are not made with an intention of making one extreme "right" and the other "wrong". They are however they are and indicative and representative of every prejudiced group. They are the Yin and Yang of the effects of prejudice. The most painful degrees of their external attack in the world is, however, representative of their own internal conflict and attack is always fear-based. As such, it does not bring a lasting peace. Like attracts like, so it must bring more of itself. It must bring more attack.

On the other hand, non-violent methods of protest are based in love, not fear. This does not mean that they do not recognize the error of prejudice. This is the very reason why they work. Dr. Martin Luther King, Jr. truly had the right idea. Influenced by Gandhi, his ideas worked well until fear-based and attacking elements took the non-violent wheels of his train off the track. Rev. King's ideas are still capable of working for African Americans and for every other group of prejudiced people.

The attacking element of all prejudiced groups makes the most noise but they do not create lasting change because their work is born of fear instead of love. It can be recognized for its good intentions but it must also be recognized as misguided, for it endeavors to raise a healthy plant without food or water as it separates from its Source and from those whom it attacks. In doing so, it shields the plant from the sun and beats the weeds close to the plant with such gusto that it damages the plant itself. It cannot offer anything of lasting value to the plant as long as it labors for it while being cut off from its Infinite Power Source of love.

The seed itself must also be strong to yield a healthy plant. Love is strong and fear is weak. This is why everyone must continue their own work on their own inner core and change it from fear to love before they can truly change their world. If *EVERYONE* would do their own work of pushing through their fears to resolve and cancel its effects upon themselves, the world would be a peaceful place. The outer world can only reflect our interior landscape.

This is also why going at it backward never works. If we look for peace and love through drugs, alcohol and/or sex, we tend to require more drugs, alcohol and/or sex and we are never quite satisfied. As Buddha said, "Craving is the cause of suffering." By seeking peace and love through work and recognition, we become workaholics with cardiac problems who fall into depression or drop dead with retirement. By seeking peace and love through relationships, we set them up to fail. It is far more effective to bring peace and love to a relationship than to seek them through the relationship.

When we seek peace and love through material possessions, we have only to become wealthy enough to satisfy even the most voracious appetite for things of the material world to know that having them has nothing to do with our experience of peace and love. Ultimately, all material seeking fails to produce them. This is what a mid-life crises is all about. Having embarked upon a quest for peace and love in all the wrong places for 40 to 50 years, we recognize that we have failed. At the same time, we cannot abandon the importance of our need to find it. This often results in our striking out in new directions. To find, we must seek. Change is always good, even though it does not always look that way. This is because the person contemplating the appearance is not also contemplating the area of Divine will. Pain is usually associated with a wound until it heals. This is the nature of the healing process.

Seeking as hard as you can, peace and love are not "out there" to be found. They are inside of you hidden only by your clouds of fear. Allow those clouds to lift through the canceling process of forgiveness and you will find that love is what you are and always were and peace is your natural expression. Permitting yourself to be what you are successfully completes your search for peace and love. It has taken you this long to find it only because you have been looking in the wrong place.

Once you find it in yourself, you are able to see it in the world. The changes which are made in your life allow for a greater reflection of the peace and love within you. This has been their purpose all along. Where fear has previously separated you from the world, love now unites you with the world. Your fear, judgment and prejudice ends and your illusions of what never was can now disappear. This allows you to know, at last, that love is what you really are and what you really want to be. Your will and the Creator's will are finally one. This allows you to clearly see that love is absolutely everywhere else to be found in your life. Why, even the places where love is not boldly evident are but crying out for love! More of it in you facilitates the healing process within you and the world. Would you withhold the help which you can offer by failing to make the recognition that love is what you are? As the *Course In Miracles* says: "Teach only love, for that is what you are."

It is time for all of us to begin a new journey in the evolvement of our consciousness and put the old, unproductive methods of the past aside. They have not worked. They have been fear-based and have encouraged us to create more fear, judgment and prejudice in ourselves and in the world. We can create a loving world by becoming more loving. Using the principle of "like attracts like" in a responsible manner, we shall create a brand new world.

As we stop being fearful, the world ceases to attack us. As we stop being fearful, we create more room for love. As love fills the space prepared for it, the contents of it create a brand new movie in our heads with a more harmonious sound track. The theme of this production becomes all of the possibilities of treating others as we, ourselves, would be treated. It looks and sounds inspiring. Our mind's projector then projects these thoughts upon the screen of life and gone are the old illusions of the past. Gone also is the pain of prejudice. As our inner core of fear changes into love, the personal movies of the past, devoid at last of the violence of fear and attack, find the peaceful resolution of a happy ending, for a change.

Let us begin this brand new journey. How exciting it is to contemplate this bold new adventure. Leaving behind the unproductive past to discover the potential of what the future holds is exactly the journey we accomplish through the canceling process of forgiveness. It opens for us a world that we never could have imagined. It takes us to a place more beautiful than any place we have ever been before. We are in the same world, but because we relate to it differently, the world is magically transformed.

Are you ready for this a brand new journey? Are you ready for a new adventure? Then, please put on your ruby red slippers for we are going to depart!

Let your imagination lift you to a higher place and whirl you off in space to set you down in a beautiful valley. It is springtime here and new growth is flowering, colorful and abundantly evident everywhere. The Goddess, Isis, is here and you are able to picture Her as a beautiful woman.

As She comes closer to you, you begin to feel more and more peaceful. Telepathically, it seems, She begins to speak to you through your mind. Intuitively, you know the thoughts that She projects as She knows yours. She says: "I am the pregnant earth, forever unfolding for you. Treat me with love and I shall provide for you always." She bids you to walk down to the edge of a beautiful lake where the water is sparkling in the sunlight, blue as lapis and crystal clear. She bids you to kneel and cup a drink of water to your mouth. As the water enters your body, you feel wonderfully energized. It feels as though some additional electric currents have entered your body. Your flesh feels lighter and lighter and you begin to hear a faint buzzing in your ears which gradually becomes a powerful inner voice. "See the mountain straight ahead? Walk across the lake and follow the path that takes you to the top." Is this the Goddess speaking? "Yes", She says, "It is I in you. You are on a journey to more of Me and more of you." Without understanding how or why, and without reservations of any kind, you begin to walk across the lake. A school of fish quickly begin to circle you on your voyage, periodically jumping, playing and showing off for you. They make clear your path as they go before you. You feel comforted and loved. While you cannot remember ever having had such an experience, it somehow feels quite natural to be walking on the water. With joy and anticipation, you continue.

Arriving at the other side, you pause to begin to say good-bye to your playmates. As you begin to speak, they magically transform themselves into birds and begin to fly with you as sentinels leading the way. You continue your journey to the top of the mountain, drinking in the beauty of the colorful flowers along the path. You are energized by the experience of the colors becoming one with you. Her breath is felt upon your forehead as Her words unfold within your mind: "It is time for you to learn about the rest of me and to know that balancing all of what I AM within you is your purpose and your work to accomplish now."

You take those last few steps which bring you to the very top. You encounter a brilliant light which warms you as you to sit down and rest awhile. As you do so, you close your eyes. You begin to meditate and pray. You are aware that you are with the Source of your being. The Goddess is with you but melting into Her is the God of the sky, as earth and air join fire and water to become more of their essence in you. The Father God begins to speak: "The world has made me much too important and it has failed to properly honor your Mother. It is time for these wounds to heal. If you heal them within yourself, you will cancel all that was before. It is time for you to be the Truth that you may know, the Truth will set you free. You see, I am lost without your Mother and She is lonely without Me. For as long as you do not unite Us within you, you will continue to look for the One who is missing in the world.

Do you understand?" You affirm your understanding and that you are ready for the journey which includes and knows the Mother-Father Source more deeply than ever before within yourself and you vow to live by this Truth.

No sooner than it takes you to phrase these thoughts in your mind, the Light begins to become more brilliant to your mind's eye. It seems to be a strange mixture of power and peace. Entering into its energy, you experience quietness within, complete and total, and at peace with all there is. The Light begins to speak:

I AM THAT I AM; I am the Tao; I am the Way, the Truth and the Life. I am Compassion; I am Forgiveness; I am Love; I am the Golden Rule. I am the Goddess; I am God; I am Yahweh; I am Christ; I am Brahman; I am Buddha; I am Isis; I am you and I am more than you. I am all the names that you have ever called me and WE ARE ONE.

If you would know My nature and know the Truth, you would also know your own nature and your own truth. It can be stated in one word and that is: LOVE. It is known and felt through your treatment of others. If you would become all that you are, you must realize and actualize LOVE to the fullest extent in your life. It is not enough to think about it, you must also practice it. Open your eyes now and look at the truth as I display it for you in its simplest written form.

> *Love is all there really is. Give it freely to*
> *everyone.*
> *Only fear gets in the way. It is but an illusion*
> *which causes you to withhold love.*
> *Value only love. It is Goddess/God and your*
> *expression of that union in yourself and in the world.*
> *Eliminate fear through forgiveness. Your river of*
> *love can then flow freely to all.*

The Light begins to slowly disperse, leaving you with new awarenesses which feel comfortable and remembered from long ago. With a feeling of expanded love and the peace it brings, you hike back down the mountain path. You can see the lake in the distance and you send your message of peace and love to the Earth Mother. You reflect upon your experience of crossing it and upon your revelations on the mountain top. You send peace and love to the Sky Father as you celebrate the two of them in you.

All of it seems like a dream. You continue along the path and you soon come to a place in the road which veers off to the right in a new direction. You decide to take it just to see where this adventure will take you. It leads you down into a quaint little town. From a distance, it looks like a Victorian village with lots of points and steep angles. It appears as a city of light.

As you arrive at its outskirts, you come to what appears to be a hot, almost bubbling spring. The misty steam beacons you to experience its warmth. You take off your clothes and immerse your body in the liquid warmth of the water as you close your eyes to contemplate the powerful happenings of the day. A brilliant light once again appears to your mind's eye. It begins as a small circle of light which grows larger and larger until it encompasses you completely. It seems to supercharge the water and your body begins to tingle. The voice of your inner teacher begins to speak:

Willingness, your willingness to try to treat all others as you would be treated is the key that opens the door to your understanding. Know that I shall be with you to guide you if you stumble as you have in the past. I shall help you just as long as you are willing. It would not be my purpose to interfere with your free will, even if it does not so align with me; however, it is the cause of your pain.

Your body is being healed right now in these waters of faith. Your mind and emotions will be healed through forgiveness. Your spirit is where we join and it is already perfect. Now, go and be the Truth of love's expression in the world, that you may become its teacher to all you meet. Stay focused upon this and only this and your blessings shall be great.

I know that you have been wondering if the events of this day are but a dream. They are not. It is all the days that came before this day which are the dream.

You reflect upon your message for a few moments and repeat to yourself: "I am willing; I am willing." Then you open your eyes to find yourself back in your earthly world. You look around and things look familiar but *you seem to experience them differently.* You feel the balance of the Mother-Father Source within you as you reflect once again upon your fantastic adventure. You understand that the meaning and purpose of your life has significantly changed. Instead of asking: "What can I get from life?" you are asking: "What can I give to life?" You have discovered that receiving is giving and you have found your way to LOVE. It expands by your treatment of others, yes, to even those who do not yet understand its meaning. Your understanding of love becomes the very bridge to their understanding and you have begun a new journey.

REFLECTIONS

Mother-Father Source of my being, help me to realize my love potential through forgiveness. Canceling my mistakes of the past will lead me to the realization that love is what I am. As I return to my recognition of my true self, I am able to more deeply express myself in the world.

I shall take every opportunity to heal the world with love through my example of its expression. Guide my every thought and action that they be based in love and become the energy expression of the Golden Rule. By realizing that love is what I am, I claim my worthiness to be treated with love and I own my responsibility to treat others with love. There are no exclusions in my understanding.

Mother-Father Source, thank You for helping me to balance You in me, for this preview of my life's new journey and for the revelations and understandings You continue to bring to me through my inner self. I am willing and I am dedicated to practicing the Truth of love.

Thank You for helping me to understand its simplicity. Give me the strength to practice it without reservation that I might help the world to heal.

So long have I sought wholeness only to stumble on fear and trip on judgment. Thank you for enabling me to see that they are but illusions no longer worthy of me. I release my past through forgiveness as I embark upon love's journey home.

CHAPTER NINE

Holy Relationships

A relationship has often been described as being full of holes or even as an unholy mess, but holy? Please! Does this not extend the realm of remote probability into the impossible? Is it really possible for any two individuals to have a relationship which could be called holy? What is a holy relationship anyway? Is it refusing to argue in front of the kids or not needing to call 911? Is it a series of dates to a prayer meeting? What, pray tell me, is a holy relationship?

A holy relationship is one which puts the relationship with the Creator first, for both parties. It is formed from an awareness that my relationship with the Source of my being is my most important relationship and that the same is true for my partner. The Source comes first and my partner comes second. The order of the rest of the things in life may be negotiated. I desire to assist you in developing your Source relationship and you desire to assist me with mine. That is really what our relationship is about even though there are many dimensions to this reality. Some of these dimensions may be sexual. Some may be parental. Some may be professional and some may be companionable. The purpose of all of them, however, is to help each other to eliminate fear and to express more love, in other words, to become more and more like the Mother-Father Source.

Both of us are able to view the Source as perfect love. We see the Mother-Father Source as our desired role model and we seek to become like the Source. Since the Source is *only* love, *perfect love* (there is no fear within the Source), this is what we desire to become. We seek to emulate this in all of our relationships with others: with our families, friends, co-workers, the homeless person on the street, the cashier at the grocery store, other drivers on the road and yes, especially with our relationship partner, be they husband, wife or same sex partner.

Our mission then becomes one of purging the many aspects of fear within us, for they stand as barriers to our experience and expression of love of self and of others. For instance, if we did not fear that homeless person on the street, we would be able to look at him or her directly, smile and radiate a little love their way. If we had no fear of failure within us, we would be able to treat our co-workers more lovingly. Fear is the only thing that stands as a barrier to love. If we could simply let go of our fears, we would let go of our irrational thoughts, judgments and prejudices against others, and we would become truly able to treat all others as we, ourselves, would be treated. In other words, we cannot live the Golden Rule until we are the Golden Rule. The Golden Rule is love and only fear stands in the way.

These are the goals of a holy relationship. Such a relationship is essentially concerned with self evolvement toward the ideal of perfect love through individual thought and expression in the world. Through balance of one's view of the Mother-Father Source, each relationship participant is committed to working on that balance within him/herself. Such is accomplished by balancing the masculine and feminine energies within oneself. As each person makes progress in balancing all that each polarity represents, they are more able to help each other. A creative female develops her logical mind. A macho male develops his sensitivity. Gone are the gender barriers which restrict balance within both genders. Balance is equally encouraged in both. If they are in a relationship together, they agree to help each other to find balance within as each one emulates the balance of the Mother-Father Source within themselves. This aligns with the directive Jesus gave us when he said that we should first love the Lord, thy God with all our hearts, and then love our neighbors as ourselves (Matthew 22: 36-40).

Holy relationships stress the importance of putting the Source first and of loving the Mother-Father Source with all our hearts. As we do so, we become *one* with that love. We are then able to express that love in the world. Until we have the experience of perfect love, we do not know how to love perfectly. It is a lot like riding a bicycle. We can have it explained to us and we can watch someone riding it but we do not *know* how to ride a bicycle until we actually ride one.

If we leave the Source out of our love equation, we sacrifice our perfect-love role model. We can still have relationships but we do not have a frame of reference for what we are seeking. These relationships soon become unholy ones which use rather than love others. We simply do not know what love is because we have not yet experienced it. We think it is "take" instead of "give". Without a balance of love within us, we cannot love in a balanced manner.

Imagine Patti, who has never done so before, trying to cross a stream by stepping on rocks irregularly placed within it. She's afraid if she loses her balance, she will fall in. She teeters her way across, lurching in various directions because she places too much of her unbalanced weight upon these stones. This is similar to what we do in our unholy relationships. Being out of balance ourselves, we lean too heavily on our partners. This has given rise to the saying: "She/he is a stone around my neck". If we increase Patti's fear by making the water deeper (let us pretend the water is 12 feet deep and the bottom is not visible), she will wobble even more so. She may allow herself to become so imbalanced that she falls into the water. In relationship vernacular, this is what is called "going off the deep end".

Relationships are all about balance, the presence and the absence of it. The relationships where it is present tend to be more harmonious and the relationships where balance is absent simply do not last very long. For as long as they last, the participants seem to be in for a bumpy ride.

The perfect holy relationship begins with two individuals who have achieved some semblance of wholeness within themselves and who are positively committed to continuing their personal work together. If they were not in this type of a relationship with each other, they would be happy to continue this work alone or until they found someone else who was also similarly committed to wholeness. It is accepted that each individual would have sifted through his/her own relationship with their Higher Power and accepted it in ways which are self-supporting and self-actualizing. The relationship with the Source or one's Higher Power then becomes the primary relationship for each individual. The relationship with his/her partner becomes one which encourages and sustains continued growth of the primary relationship for each individual. Their relationship with each other becomes the secondary relationship. This keeps each relationship participant from leaning too heavily upon the other. While the relationship is still mutually satisfying for both, it is not dependent upon the other. Personal growth can then be further facilitated through free flowing and honest communication.

In other words, "My relationship with the Source of my being is my most important relationship and I accept that your relationship with your Higher Power is your most important relationship." Our personal relationship will support our Source-centered primary relationships by providing each of us the opportunity to continue letting go of fear. This is the purpose of all of our relationships. By doing so, we become more loving to each other and to all others through our life's expression, the ideal of which brings the Golden Rule into action in our lives. We agree to use forgiveness as a tool for letting go of fear and we anticipate that progress will be found through our willingness to communicate with each other.

We are willing to commit to each other, to stay in the relationship to help each other heal, to listen to each other, share ourselves, love and emotionally support each other no matter how things appear to be in the moment. We agree to continue to release our fears and to communicate about this release with each other. We agree to do so forever or for just as long as the relationship serves to strengthen our primary relationship with our Source. We agree to continue to emotionally support our relationship as we continue growing in our understanding of love as our true nature and we continue to progress in our ability to express love instead of fear. These are the commitments we are willing to make to each other. Such is the essence of a holy relationship.

It seems fair to say that most people, be they heterosexual or homosexual, do not have holy relationships. If a person begins a relationship with no concept of the importance of individual wholeness, he/she looks to the relationship partner to complete his/her missing parts. "Together, we shall be whole" never works unless there is first an individual commitment to personal wholeness. This is one of the most important reasons why relationships fail.

Many relationships begin with sexual attraction yet history attests to the fact that sex cannot sustain a relationship if there are not other, more important foundations on which to build. Sexual relations in a holy relationship are secondary to personal growth but they are also satisfying and promote intimacy. Communication helps to minimize separation and amplify the intensity of the sexual experience. The quality of the experience becomes more important than the focus upon frequency. It is mostly because of increased mental and emotional separation that sexuality diminishes. When this occurs, relationships which are primarily based on sexual attraction fail.

Where does this concept of separation begin? It begins long before the relationship. If a person feels separate from the Source of his/her being and separated from the world, separation becomes an understanding which is easily accepted and promoted in the life of the individual and in his/her relationships. Fear is at the root of separation. Where fear exists, love cannot be. This is true of all relationships, be they heterosexual or homosexual in nature, although some aspects seem to be more amplified for homosexuals.

As a group, many homosexuals tend to separate from the Source of their being because they believe, at some level, the prejudicial beliefs held by others about them. That "they are not worthy" or "are going straight to hell" are examples of ideas they must undo. These fear-based beliefs about their Higher Power must be dispelled in order to be able to cultivate a healthy relationship with the Source of their being, one which lovingly supports them. Otherwise, fear will become a barrier to the love of the Source and ultimately, to love of self. These barriers will further strengthen the concept of separation within them. Likewise, if one feels a closeness with a loving Creator, one will tend to feel less separated from others, less fearful and more willing to communicate who they are and what they are feeling. In other words, loving the Source helps them in the loving process.

Fear is the major culprit in our proclivity to mentally and emotionally separate from our partner in a relationship. Fear says, "If they really know me, they will not like what they know and they will reject me." Fear's beliefs thus create barriers to love. This is why we must face our fears and push through them, to eliminate love's barriers. It is difficult for a fearful person to have a loving relationship. Fear restricts our self expression and limits the depth and quality of our relationship. To minimize separation in our relationship, we must be willing to fully express our feelings in a loving way without taking fear of rejection too seriously. We must be willing to take a risk. This is why a personal commitment to releasing fear is so important in every holy relationship. Without it, the relationship cannot grow beyond fear's barriers.

For example, Arthur and Karen become college sweethearts. Arthur comes from a poor family and he is working his way through college. Karen comes from an affluent family who has everything. Arthur and Karen's relationship develops, and after graduation, they decide to get married. They have three wonderful children.

Arthur has fears of inadequacy which did not begin with Karen. His interaction with Karen does, however, allow him to see these fears. Arthur's fears began long ago when he made an invalid association that material affluence equals self worthiness. He must now choose what to do about these feelings. Arthur may decide to talk openly with Karen about his fears (actually, he could have decided to do this long ago). To do so, he must allow himself to be vulnerable and to risk rejection. Another alternative is to decide to ignore these feelings and avoid conversation about his fears.

Cultural and gender conditioning make it easy for him to opt for the latter. Maybe these fears will go away as he becomes more successful in the world. Arthur carries these fears of inadequacy with him and seems to fail at everything he tries, which then enables him to feel even more inadequate. He begins to numb the pain with alcohol as he becomes more and more mentally, emotionally and physically distant from his family.

Karen threatens to leave him if he does not change. His interpretation of this permits him to feel even more inadequate and to drink more. His fears and his behavior, in order to cope with them, lead to a break in the relationship as Karen leaves (with the children) the man she loves to protect her own sanity and the psyche of their children.

This ultimate actualization of his fear allows Arthur to bottom out, find Alcoholics Anonymous and get in touch with his Higher Power. This process leads to communication 101 or "getting real". As long as Arthur remains willing to change for the better, cultivates his relationship with the Source (his Higher Power) and works the forgiveness process (AA has its own excellent method), love is able to replace fear within him. Arthur then becomes able to love and forgive himself and others. When he has done enough of this to remove his fears of inadequacy (which he is able to do by talking about them), he is able to change his beliefs about them. He becomes more capable of experiencing and expressing love or of living by the Golden Rule. He then becomes capable of having a holy relationship.

If Karen is willing and he also desires to do so, they can try again. This new relationship has the opportunity to be more communicative, intimate and loving. With less fear, there is more room for love. If they opt not to try again with each other, Arthur now has the ability to have a successful and holy relationship with someone else just as long as he remains willing to replace his fears with love. He also now has a primary Source relationship to help him to do so. He need not ever lean so heavily on his partner again.

Those of you reading this book, who realize your own personal problems with alcohol (or drugs), consider picking up the phone and calling the AA Hotline now. The problem will not go away until you deal with it. Until you have done so, your fears can only gather more energy, rendering you incapable of having a holy relationship. There is a Power greater than yourself that is available to you now. As you develop your Source relationship, develop your ability to change your irrational beliefs about yourself and the world and, last but not least, develop your ability to forgive yourself and others, you are on the way to restoring yourself to love.

It is the growth of fear in relation to the self and the Creator which contribute to relationship demise. In like manner, love expression and love growth allows relationships to flourish. Love expands and fear contracts. Love multiplies and fear subtracts. Love creates light and fear creates darkness. This speaks of the very meaning of life itself in its simplest form. Our life's creativity always creates more of the essence of itself in all of our relationships. Love cannot create fear and fear cannot create love.

We do have personal choice. We have the free will to choose as we see fit but we should be mindful that the only choice we are ever really making is the one between love and fear. A holy relationship chooses love and, because it does, it continues to grow, even beyond the rough times which are certainly there in all relationships. A holy relationship continues to become more like the Source and its participants more like the expression of the Creator in the world. A holy relationship becomes the Golden Rule in its intent and through its action in the world.

We have so far explored what this holy relationship is like and the major pitfalls in not having a holy relationship. Now we shall more deeply explore the mechanics of how it works in a lesbian relationship. Jane and Mary meet at a dance. They feel an immediate attraction and agree to see more of each other. After many dates, they become sexually intimate. A month later, they decide to begin living together. Jane has already come to terms with who she is. She is "out" to her parents and her family and to some friends at work. She is currently contemplating "coming out" to her employer. Mary is totally "in the closet" and has great fear around her identity. Does their relationship have a chance to make it? The answer can be yes or no.

If both women are committed to overcoming fear and helping each other to do so, the relationship has an opportunity for growth. Jane has already begun to unravel the fear associated with her nature and identity. Her example can serve as an opportunity for Mary to grow or it can serve to make Mary even more fearful. If Mary accepts the former, she will begin learning to let go of fear. It may happen slowly but it will happen progressively and surely. Mary's choice will help to further influence Jane in her process of letting go of fear.

If Mary accepts the latter and becomes even more fearful because of Jane's behavior of letting go of fear associated with her nature as a lesbian, this will cause both of them to begin to separate, mentally and emotionally, from the relationship. Jane will separate because her knowledge regarding the dissolution of fear feels too good to abandon. She would not go back to the closet of fear because she has a frame of reference for experiencing what it is like to let go of fear. She must continue on that path. Mary will separate because she has no frame of reference for being without this fear and she is unwilling to take the risk to find out. Fear of the unknown maintains her status quo. It is only a matter of time until the mental and emotional separation will be complete and the relationship will be broken.

We could play out a similar scenario in every relationship using different examples of fear and similarly conclude that every relationship has the opportunity to grow if both parties are committed to letting go of fear. When an impasse is reached by one or both, the separation process will begin. There is no end to the kind of fears each party may have when he/she begins a relationship. It really does not matter what the fear is and it is important to realize that whatever one's fear is, it has nothing to do with the other person. One person may have experienced sexual abuse and is therefore afraid of sexuality in some way. Their feelings really have nothing to do with their relationship partner. Another person may have a fear of failure because of parental pressure and punishment for making less than an "A" on their report cards. Someone else may have a fear of intimacy because they were once betrayed.

The point is this: All of us have fears about something. It is our choice to maintain our fears and allow them to grow or to release them and allow ourselves to grow. Our fears are always about us and never about our partner. If we are not willing to release our fears, when our relationship partner comes too close to that fear through thought, word or deed, we shall begin retreating and shutting down, mentally and emotionally. This signals the beginning of the separation process and the demise of our relationship. It is our willingness to let go of fear and to grow personally which allows us to grow in our relationships. The Source of our being can then help us with this process.

Both parties in the relationship must be willing or relationship growth cannot unfold. If I am willing and you are not, then when I grow as much as possible with you, I shall need to separate to continue my growth. If you are not willing to grow, then you will need to try again with someone else. What a coincidence it seems to be when the next person gives you the very same opportunities for growth. This is when you might conclude: "There must be something here that I am not learning." Falling "out of love" is often little more than falling "into fear".

Every relationship has the opportunity to grow stronger in its love component but only if both parties are willing to release their fears. Since there is only love and fear, releasing fear allows love its opportunity for growth. Sometimes we are willing but the fear is so deep and so strong within us that we need help in releasing it. This is the purpose for bringing the Source greater than ourselves into the picture, to provide us with the help we need to release those fears. This is the way we grow and it is therefore important we avail ourselves of all the help we need in order to get the job done. This is why a holy relationship is so effective. Each participant has constant and total availability to Power beyond their limited, fearful self. Such Power allows for risk taking when needed, when the lack of such Power might result in immobilization.

Therefore, my primary relationship must affirm my openness to my Higher Power, and your primary relationship to yours. Each one will then have a way to get unstuck when needed as I release my fears and you release yours and, together, we help each other in the process. The purpose of a holy relationship is to more effectively release fear and to more efficiently yield personal growth in the ability to love. As long as these results continue for both parties, the relationship thrives. Both parties become more able to experience and express love because love is recognized as the absence of fear.

The more fear we release, the more willing we are to communicate our feelings to our partner. A relationship cannot sustain itself and grow without this. It is what a healthy relationship is all about. The communication process is what helps each other to continue releasing fear and sharing the process. Each party in the relationship then becomes the teacher to the other, the catalyst for releasing pain, a vulnerability model and an example of the Golden Rule by treating his/her partner the way he/she would like to be treated. This strengthens and allows for more love to manifest within the relationship and this permits a holy relationship. To review, its components are as follows:

1. My relationship with my Source is my most important relationship because opening to Power beyond my limited self is important and sometimes mandatory to my ability to release my fears.

2. Releasing my fears and communicating with you on this process allows me to help you release your fears and become more communicative with me about your feelings.

3. I am willing to be vulnerable with you and I want you to be vulnerable with me as we continue our work. Let there be not one single thing we feel unable to share with each other.

4. You are my second most important relationship and I desire to be yours. I shall not make you more or less important and this is exactly what I want from you.

5. I commit to the daily use of meditation, prayer, the use of the Prejudice releasing process in Chapter 1, the Forgiveness instrument explained in Chapter 6 and/or other tools for personal growth. Let us both agree to share our thoughts and ideas regarding these processes.

6. I totally commit to this relationship with you forever for as long as we are both committed to doing our personal work as defined in #1-5. The one goal of our relationship is to release all of our fears so we may create more room for love.

Does this sound like the type of relationship you would like to have? Then begin preparing yourself by strengthening your primary relationship in a manner acceptable to you. By affirming your willingness, you will be led to the next step. Listen to your inner guidance. It may lead you to do some inspirational reading or to a house of worship. It may lead you to a therapist or to a twelve step program. It may lead you to another line of work, to another town or even to another relationship. Once you affirm your desire to strengthen your relationship with your primary Source, you must also be willing to take action upon the guidance you receive. Do not worry that it seems to manifest through your imagination. This is often the way the Source speaks to us. Act upon it and more guidance will be forthcoming. The Source's directives will always be positive, loving and helpful courses of action for you. They shall always be about you and they shall never be about harming others.

As you begin the strengthening of your primary relationship, begin also to work with releasing prejudice as presented through the four step model in Chapter 1 and with the forgiveness process by using the instrument presented in Chapter 6. This will help you begin to release the fears which are your barriers to the experience and expression of love. It will also put you in touch with the origin of these fears which will surely surprise you from time to time, for the origin is often not within our conscious awareness and not what we think it is. Give thanks to the Source of your being for all the progress that you make. Your willingness to change and your gratitude for progress made will amplify your future results.

If you are already in a relationship, perhaps your partner is willing to join you in these adventures. If not, do not allow this to discourage you from beginning. You may find that continued exposure to the ideas in this book may be helpful. You may want to read and re-read it until you feel you have a grasp of the work presented and it is workable for you. The ideas are offered as methods which may be helpful to you in attaining wholeness.

Your wholeness is important not only to you but also to the world. The more wholeness everyone is able to find within themselves and within their relationships, the more able they are to help the world to heal.

Using the holy relationship model for growth within our personal lives strengthens our ability to use it in the world. Our willingness to communicate, to be vulnerable and to experience ourselves being strengthened as we learn to release our fears, will give us the courage to step out on faith and help the world through our example. When we become willing, Mother-Father Source will guide us on how and what we are to do.

"How do we actually practice the Golden Rule in our relationships? What about the times my partner makes me angry?" If we accept that there is only love and fear, then every response we have which is less than love is a fearful one. It is appropriate material for use by the prejudice releasing model in Chapter 1 and by the forgiveness instrument given in Chapter 6. These may lead you to the real reason for your distress which has nothing to do with your partner. You are never upset for the reason you think. Once you have gotten to the bottom of this for yourself, share your revelations with your partner. "I recognize that my anger had nothing to do with you. What you said triggered some memories of my past which were the cause of my upset. This is what I have discovered about them . . ."

Are you prepared to accept that all of your negative emotional responses in your relationships are only about you? If not, then you are destined to continue experiencing them over and over again. If this appears to be happening, you may want to consider ordering Dr. Michael Ryce's taped workshop: *Why Is This Happening To Me Again?* or his book by the same title. See references.

If you are ready for 100 % personal responsibility, you are ready to employ the ideas in *Barriers To Love*. As you begin your work and begin to see the results of more love and less fear in your relationship with your significant other, you might begin to use the very same principles and processes for all of the other relationships in your life. Your friendships and your professional relationships will all benefit from this procedure. As you work with this process, you will find yourself healing memories of the past, many of which you will find are based in your parental relationships.

Working with forgiveness to achieve and maintain holy relationships with everyone will enable you to do your part by becoming a personal example of the Golden Rule. In becoming so, you will have developed a strong relationship with the Source of your being, through which all things are possible. You will have transformed the energy of your fears, almost miraculously, into love. You will have learned to take risks in the communication process.

If you are heterosexual, you find yourself without prejudice for those different from yourself and more able to be loving and accepting of everyone who strives to live ethically, treating others as they would be treated. If you are homosexual, you may then look as hard as you can and you will not be able to find a "closet" that would contain you. Because you are free from fear at last, you believe that you are worthy of ethical treatment from others. Instead of hiding, you will eagerly open yourself to receive love and acceptance from the world as you uphold your part of the bargain by treating others as you would like to be treated. This openness of who you are and your ethical treatment of others will do more to eliminate prejudice against homosexuals than all the rhetoric in the world.

Attacking the world cannot work because attack is based in fear. It can only create more fear. Let everyone now resolve to heal the world with love as we go forward to create holy relationships in our lives and respect for all others. This will lead us to holy relationships in the world.

REFLECTIONS

Mother-Father Source of my being, I am ready to learn how to have a holy relationship. I am ready to put these principles into action so that I might begin living by the Golden Rule. Guide me in this process.

I shall begin by strengthening my relationship with You and making it the most important relationship in my life. From it, my strength will spring to release all of my fears and return myself to my natural state of love.

Mother-Father Source, I open myself to a holy relationship with my significant other and I commit myself to personal growth, that we might grow together in expressing You in our life together and in the world. May we both be open to releasing our fears together. If this cannot be, then guide us both to a relationship where this becomes possible.

Source of my being, I shall use prayer, meditation and the forgiveness instrument daily to affirm my willingness to have a holy relationship. I shall listen to Your voice within me and I shall act upon Your guidance. Thank you Mother-Father Source for Your help in my life.

CHAPTER TEN

Finding Your Light

"Why am I here? What am I supposed to be doing with my life? What is it that will truly make me happy?" Everyone has asked these questions at some time in their lives. We all desire to find our *divine purpose* in life. We have also been told to "seek and ye shall find" and we certainly have been looking for it. "Where, for heaven's sake, is it?"

Seeking this elusive goal, we have sought our *divine purpose* through work and through relationships. The vast majority of us have not found it there. Bill may have stayed in a job he hated for thirty years and Pam may have remained in a lifeless marriage for fifty years. Many others have imitated them as they claimed their share of stress-related disorders and diseases. Could this possibly be their *divine purpose* in life? I don't think so!

If wherever you are does not feel good, you have not found your *divine purpose* in life. If you do not flow like a river with the space that you occupy, you have not found it yet. If your life's work or your relationships feel more like you are swimming upstream against a profoundly strong current, consider this to be a clue from the universe. If it were your *divine purpose*, you would flow with it effortlessly. Somehow, you took a wrong turn in the maze of life and you just might be pig-headed enough to be unwilling to recognize your mistake for what it is. You want to be right and you are determined to be right, even if it kills you! Are you also prepared to accept the fact that it might do just that?

Meet the moment of truth by asking yourself: "Do I flow like a river with the work that I am doing? Is it the work I would do even if I were not paid for doing it? Does time fly by when I am doing my work? Does my work energize me or does it make me feel tired? Does my work make me joyous or depressed?" If money is the main reason that you do the work you do, and time moves very slowly when you are at work, this is important feedback for you to consider. If your work totally depletes your energy, mentally, emotionally and physically, and you arrive and leave in a depressed state, you are not experiencing your *divine purpose* in life as it relates to your work. So, stop trying to make it right, even if it kills you! Is money really worth more than your peace of mind?

The purpose of the last chapter was to give you some ideas to implement so that this can begin to happen for you. Relationships should feel good and holy relationships do. Cultivating them can lead you to your *divine purpose* in life. If you and your partner are committed to having a holy relationship, you then have the Source of your being and your partner to help you to find your *divine purpose* in life. Your interaction with both of them will provide you with a rudder for your ship and wind for your sails in this voyage called life. They shall comfort you as you learn to flow with the currents instead of fighting them. You have already charted your course long ago and the currents naturally move you in this direction.

If it were not for the value that you place on money, how would your life be different? Has it kept you swimming upstream against the currents? How tired have you allowed yourself to become? Working with someone in a holy relationship will help you toward your truth, the one which allows you to take risks to arrive at a state of freedom. You and the Source are there to help your partner do the same.

As you begin to release your fears and become more loving, as you begin to "get real" in your communication with others, as you begin to help others to heal by healing yourself, you will most surely be guided to your *divine purpose* in life. Beginning with you, it will then extend outward to all others and all things in your life. The key to having good relationships with everyone and everything is achieved by becoming good relationship material and this is what you become as you return to your natural state of love. From this state of consciousness you are able to fulfill your responsibilities to the Golden Rule. Without personal growth, the Golden Rule remains forever an altruistic idea which, try as hard as you may, you just are not able to practice. This can only bring frustration and guilt, both of which inhibit you from flowing like a river with your *divine purpose* in life.

Having holy relationships with everyone is your *divine purpose* in relationships. Doing your work in this regard will not allow you to remain in a lifeless marriage or union for fifty years. The fact that it is lifeless can only be because two people are unwilling to do their work. If even one of them decides to become willing to work in personal healing, the relationship will change. If this should stimulate willingness in the other, the relationship will begin to breathe in new life and it will grow. If one doing his/her work fails to stimulate willingness in the other, the relationship will die.

Willingness is always the key to growth and growth always stimulates change. So, how do you feel about change? Do you avoid it whenever possible? Do you resist it? It is often our resistance to change which keeps us from fulfilling our *divine purpose* in life. Resistance is born of fear instead of love. Be mindful that change does not necessarily mean that we must change partners unless they happen to be resistant to our own positive change. This misperception seems to happen often in relationships and may play itself out more frequently in homosexual relationships because of the lack of legal ties as would be found in heterosexual marriages, although one out of every two marriages ending in divorce is certainly nothing to emulate. We shall deal with the volatile issue of gay marriage in the next chapter. Divorce or separation in emotional partnership may speak of resistance to change and/or to positive personal growth within one or both of the individuals involved. Whatever the situation, the marriage does not fail; the people do.

The reason that we seek and seek and never find our *divine purpose* in relationships is because we are looking in the wrong place. We cannot find it by looking outside ourselves. We cannot find it in other people and we cannot arrive there by fault finding and blaming others. We can find it through our own implementation of the Golden Rule, as we flow with the currents of life. We cannot arrive at this destination without a willingness to release our fears and to return ourselves to love. It is always fear which keeps us from finding our *divine purpose* in life through our relationships.

When you learn to make your relationships holy, you are on the path to finding your *divine purpose*. You will recognize the truth of this by how your relationships feel. Holy relationships feel good, even through their growing pains, and they always treat others with dignity and respect because they are a positive application of the Golden Rule. Because this is so, this is what they bring you in return. You already have a frame of reference for how to go about creating holy relationships, but what about the rest of your *divine purpose* in life? What about your life's work? What work are you supposed to be doing? What kind of work will really make you happy? Could it be that the kind of work you are supposed to be doing is the kind of work that will make you happy? What a grand idea!

As we explore this idea further, let us digress for a moment to the meaning of life and our purpose for being here. We are here for one purpose and one purpose alone. We are here to learn to love the Source of our being with all our hearts and we are here to learn to love our neighbors as ourselves. We can further distill this by saying that we are here to learn to love. It is the practice of the Golden Rule which allows us to learn this lesson. If we cannot practice it, we cannot learn it.

Think for a moment about how business and industry tend to operate in a materialistic society and it will give you some insight on how we are failing to learn the lesson of love through work. No wonder it is so difficult to find our *divine purpose* of life through work. The problem results from a misperception of the goal of work. Is the goal of work love or money? If we perceive that our satisfaction with work is related to the amount of money the work generates, then we cannot achieve our *divine purpose* in life through the work we do. It will usually take just a little more money to make us happy. Once we arrive there, we find that a little more would be better and so on. It guides us to the adoption of the philosophy: "More is better!" This philosophy leads us to addiction which is always thirsty and never quite satisfied.

We shall find our *divine purpose* in work when we learn to work with love as part of our daily business and as the end goal of work. Think of what a different world this would be if the end goal of work for everyone were love instead of money. There would be no politics at work. There would be no jealousy or back stabbing in the work environment. Instead of employers asking: "How little can I get by with giving my workers?", they would be asking: "How much can I afford to give my workers while still making a reasonable profit?" Instead of employees asking: "How little can I get by with doing?", they would ask: "How can I improve my work so that our company can better succeed? How may I help my co-workers?" Making love the end goal of work is what creates a winning team spirit which becomes synergistic and creates more for all.

In reality, the bottom line success of the workplace is inexorably tied to the employers' and the participants' definition of the end goal of work. If this goal is to only make money, then employer and employee can never fulfill their *divine purpose* through work because they do not work with love as the major motivation. It is a very good example of not being able to serve two masters. So, let us begin asking ourselves the question: "Do we practice the Golden Rule at work?" If not, we might question which master we are serving. We may also be able to predict the results.

Finding our *divine purpose* in life through work has more to do with the way we work than with the kind of work we do. If we work with love, we enjoy our work. If we focus only upon the amount of money created by the work, we soon lapse into a chorus of Peggy Lee's song, "Is That All There Is?" Granted, it is easier for us do some jobs more easily than others, but if we could do whatever job is given us to do with love, our Higher Power could then lead us to our next step.

Many of us remain in a job that is difficult for us to do with love because of fear. We are afraid that if we leave this job, we shall not find another one that will pay as much. This should make perfectly clear to us our definition of the end goal of work. Letting go of fear could become the catalyst for positive change if we were only able to do so. If we could overcome our fears, we could seek and find another environment where we might work with love.

Doing our personal healing through forgiveness and the cultivation of holy relationships helps us to find our *divine purpose* in life by helping us to overcome our fears. Once we overcome fear in one area, it is easier to conquer it in another. Inherent in the process of overcoming is the cultivation of our relationship with the Power in the universe greater than ourselves. Learning to communicate through prayer and meditation builds our trust. Knowing that we can overcome our fears and doing so makes way for the expression of more love in our lives. This enables us to more easily practice the Golden Rule. As we do so, we cease to swim upstream and we allow ourselves to flow with the river of life having the Source as our navigator. This is how we find our *divine purpose* in life.

To put it a different way, living life is like being in school. To complete life 101, we must finish high school. This does not mean becoming proficient in reading, writing and arithmetic. High school means the evolvement to a higher level of being, a living of the total life experience from the vibration of love. It means that we no longer confuse love with sex, money or anything of the material world. It does not mean we do not have sex, money and things of the material world, but that we do not confuse them with love. It also means that we are able to realize and actualize our definition of love as the ethical treatment of others. As we do so, we become more of what we are. We mystically merge with the Creator and become the embodiment and expression of the Mother-Father Source in the world.

These ideas are appropriate ideals for all people. This is life 101 and it is safe to say that most of us have not yet learned its lessons. While heterosexuals and homosexuals have different challenges in this learning experience, a greater challenge may exist for homosexuals. As a group, they tend to experience less love from the world. Their secret life also tends to disallow them to give love to the world in an open, honest manner. In return, they receive less love. Regrettably, it is understandable for much of their lives revolves around fear. Fear avoidance only creates more fear in their lives. It is but another way to swim against the current. No matter how hard they try, fear cannot create the energy of love, for like still attracts like.

If they would be whole, homosexuals must overcome their fears regarding their identity. This will allow them to have holy relationships with the world which are loving and giving as they treat others as they would be treated. Homosexuals can resolve now to make of their lives a grand example of having learned the lesson of love by freely giving it to the world. This is part of their *divine purpose* in life. It is up to them to choose whether or not they shall take the high road on the path of life's forgiveness.

As a prejudiced group, women also have special challenges as they find their way to their *divine purpose* in life. They can spend their energies pointing out the inequities of the past (there are certainly plenty of them), or they can focus their energies on being here now. As they develop a deeper relationship with the Mother-Father Source, they allow themselves an opportunity to be healed and balanced in a way they have not experienced for at least 2000 years. As they learn to depend upon their relationship with the Source more than upon another human being, women shall allow themselves to flow with the river of life instead of swimming upstream, trying to make impossible relationships work. This will also keep them from leaning too heavily upon their relationship counterparts.

As women strengthen their faith in the Source to provide for them and agree to participate in only those relationships which are holy, their partners will come to better understand their own purpose. Knowing their purpose as exactly the same allows them to strive to experience and to express only love in the world.

All prejudiced groups have the opportunity to heal the world with love if they so desire or to perpetuate more fear in the world. It is part of everyone's *divine purpose* in life to choose love. It is a joyous undertaking which feels good. It is timeless and the time for more of it is now. Love is the longing of life itself which we fulfill by first experiencing it within our own minds and hearts. As we become love, we treat others as we would be treated (no matter how they treat us). We then become an example for a different way of being in the world, as we become a light upon their darkened path.

"Becoming *light*" is a blessing to all prejudiced groups and to all those who would oppress them. In the moment that you started your new journey, you began your journey into *light*. Having experienced the *light* within yourself has brought you to a new understanding of the *light* as something inside of you. No more can you adhere to a concept of God as "Big Daddy in the sky". This has ended forever your feeling of separation from the Mother-Father Source and it allows you to more boldly and brilliantly reflect the *light*. You have acquired a deeper awareness of who you are and with it comes a deeper understanding of the connectedness of all life. We are all doing what we are doing until we learn better. Becoming *light* is part of the journey. You read Matthew 5: 14-16 and you perceive meaning which previously was not there for you.

> Ye are the light of the world. A city that is set on
> a hill cannot be hid.
> Neither do men (*and women*) light a candle, and put it
> under a bushel, but on a candlestick; and it giveth light unto
> all that are in the house.
> Let your light so shine before men (*and women*), that
> they may see your good works, and glorify your Father
> (*and Mother*) which is in heaven.

You, yes, YOU are the *light* of the world. *Light* is the essence of the Source, the expression of which is the right treatment of all others in the world, yes, even those who would oppress you. *Light* is the Golden Rule and you are *light* in action. You are a city on the hill; you are on the mountain top and you cannot hide. Come out with acceptance of yourself in love, not fear. Let the world see the wonderful person that you are. Your *light* will help the rest of the world to become *light* as they also learn to live by the Golden Rule. You would not light a candle and put it in the closet, would you? That would defeat its purpose of bringing light. You would place it on a candlestick out in the open that it may give light to everyone in your house. You are that *light* and your house is your world. So, let the fact that you are *light* be known through letting the world know who you are, that they may see you as the love that you are. That you are *light* will be evident through your treatment of others. Let your *light* glorify the Mother-Father Source by becoming It's expression in the world.

As you remember Mark 4: 24-25, you are able to finally understand it.

> And he said unto them, Take heed what you hear:
> with what measure ye mete, it shall be measured to you:
> and unto you that hear shall more be given: and he that
> hath not, from him shall be taken even that which he
> hath.

You understand that the Master Teacher was saying that you should understand the importance of practicing the Golden Rule for you shall surely reap what you sow. If you are able to hear and understand this and are willing to try to practice it, a greater level of understanding will be given to you. However, if you understand the importance of the Golden Rule and fail to practice it, even that understanding which you have will be taken away. You must practice love, not hate and become *light*, not darkness. As you become the *light*, more *light* shall be given to you.

> He that saith he is in the light, and hateth his brother,
> is in darkness even until now.
> He that loveth his brother abideth in the light, and
> there is none occasion of stumbling in him.
> But he that hateth his brother is in darkness, and
> walketh in darkness, and knoweth not whither he
> goeth, because that darkness hath blinded his eyes.
> 1 John 2: 9-11

If we believe John, the apostle of love, we understand love more fully as *light*, the *light* we must become in the world. In doing so, we willingly release the past along with all of the oppressions we perceived when we were powerless. They were but mournful cries from those unwilling to express their *light*. We understand the pain of that resistance for we also stood upon that ground until we found a better way to be. We now release all of our fears of the past.

Women are able now to see the symbol of their fears as their sad search for approval and freedom from oppression in a world of patriarchy. Finding the *light* within themselves, they release their need for the approval of others.

Homosexuals are able to see the symbol of their fears as the "closet" which once contained them before they came out into the *light* to claim the truth of what they are. Homosexuals are even able to understand that at least one purpose for their visit to this earth plane as a homosexual was to help their brothers and sisters to find the *light*. They are willing to help them to do so through their example as they reveal their nature to others, that all might learn the lesson of judging not.

Reflecting for a moment upon the remembrance of the most profound example shown to all of us by one of the Master Teachers of the world, one incapable of judging because there was no error in him, we are able to know and understand the meaning of the truth. He was totally able to live as *light* and to show us the way.

> Jesus went into the mount of Olives.
> And early in the morning he came again into the
> temple, and all the people came unto him; and he sat
> down, and taught them.
> And the scribes and the Pharisees brought unto him
> a woman taken in adultery; and when they had set her in
> the midst,
> They say unto him, Master, this woman was taken in
> adultery, in the very act.
> Now Moses in the law commanded us, that such
> should be stoned: but what sayest thou?
> This they said, tempting him, that they might have
> to accuse him. But Jesus stooped down, and with his
> finger wrote on the ground, *as though he heard them
> not*. So when they continued asking him, he lifted up
> himself, and said unto them, He that is without sin

among you, let him first cast a stone at her.
And again he stooped down, and wrote on the
ground.
And when they heard it, being convicted by *their own
conscience*, went out one by one, beginning at the eldest,
even unto the last: and Jesus was left alone, and the
woman standing in the midst.
When Jesus had lifted up himself, and saw none but
the woman, he said unto her, Woman, where are those
thine accusers? hath no man condemned thee?
She said, No man, Lord. And Jesus said unto her,
Neither do I condemn thee: go, and sin no more.
John 8: 1-11

We understand now that those whom were intent on throwing stones were only responding to the error within themselves which was called sin. We know the meaning of sin at last: the personal error within which inhibits the full and complete expression of *light* at all times through the right treatment of others. When Jesus brought this to their soul's attention, the realization of what was really going on caused them to turn and depart. Their attack, which was based in fear, brought guilt. At the moment of this awareness, the opportunity was there to allow their fear to change to love through forgiveness. What each one chose to do we cannot know, but we can speculate that many chose darkness instead of *light* because of the prejudice and violence which still exists in the false name of righteousness.

Prejudice against women and homosexuals are but two examples of personal error so great within the oppressor that they must be projected out into the world. These oppressors are to be pitied, not attacked, for they suffer from an illness born of personal error and anger that would consume them unless they are willing to find their way to the *light*. Until they can become the expression of it through the practice of the Golden Rule, with no exclusions, they cannot know the peace of the Mother-Father Source.

Then spake Jesus again unto them, saying, I am the
light of the world: he that followeth me shall not walk
in darkness, but shall have the light of life.
John 8: 12

All prejudiced groups can help the world to heal its prejudice by themselves becoming *light* through proper acceptance of personal responsibility. If our thoughts and actions are not worthy of the *light*, we have

129

no one to blame but ourselves. We are all worthy and let us claim that as the truth about ourselves as all of us learn to live ethically, without exclusion of anyone. Let all prejudiced groups not waste another moment in blaming others for those who would oppress must answer for their own thoughts and deeds. Let everyone take the initiative to heal prejudice in the world by overcoming their own fears so that everyone becomes an example of *light* in the world. In a lecture at a Vedanta Center, Swami Adiswarananda once so succinctly said:

> "You cannot overcome darkness by fighting
> but by bringing light."

Let the wisdom of these words become real in each individual heart as the world itself and everyone in it returns to love. Finding love as one's *divine purpose* in life and becoming *light* in the world properly supports the human drama to become more of itself.

Suppose the whole world is but a stage and life is but a play? There would not be another soul who could possibly play your part in this drama. You and your life's expressions are unique in all this world. If you were to waste your energy in attack because of the injustices of a patriarchal world, would that not enable you to become just like patriarchy? If you were to hide in the closet, would this not diminish your expression? The world needs you. It cannot benefit from your uniqueness if you place your *light* "under a bushel". Would you avoid sharing your expression in a positive context if you were not afraid? As we have seen, fears can only be mere rationalizations for false beliefs. It is time to undo all of them.

It is time for women to reject the irrational thoughts men have about them. It is time for women to realize that such thoughts say more about the men who have them than they do about the women they mistreat. There is great power in the knowledge that the moment men cease to fear women, their irrational thoughts about them must change. As men realize that they can trust women with their vulnerability, men can heal their invalid cultural lessons from patriarchy. Some have already begun to do so.

There is one thing which can stop the progress made so far, and that is women getting in their face determined to make them pay for the errors of their forefathers. This is the mistake which many African Americans have made. This kind of attack can only bring more of itself. It is quite another thing to insist upon their accountability for their own deeds. It is likely that honorable men will join women in this endeavor. Likewise, if African Americans focused upon accountability from whites in relation to their own personal actions, instead of upon retribution from the white race for mistakes of the past, honorable and ethical white people (there are many) shall be right there with them. How women and African Americans choose to play their parts in life's drama is a matter of personal choice; however, their choices will lead to increased attack or to peace and love. Like shall always attract like. You are the actor in your drama. How will you play your part?

It is also time for all homosexuals to put aside beliefs that personal choice has anything to do with their Source-given nature; however, personal choice has everything to do with the manner in which they express their nature. It is time for homosexuals to accept their nature as the Creator's will, to be who they are, living openly, honestly and ethically and to play their part in the drama which the Mother-Father Source created. This play is called *Healing The Consciousness Of Humanity*.

If you refuse to play your part, humanity will be unable to heal its prejudicial thoughts about homosexuality. If you choose to remain hidden, the world will find it more difficult to heal its homophobic thoughts and beliefs. Yes, *you* are important to the achievement of this goal. If you refuse to play your part, the world will continue to be afraid of you and you will continue to be afraid of it. This will further propel you into hiding from the world.

Homosexuals must somehow get past the immobilizing fear of teeth chattering and knees knocking as they stand in the wings of life's theater. They must proclaim that they are also a child of the Creator. They must push through fear to go on stage because all of the other players need them as a catalyst for the evocation of consciousness healing. Yes, there may be some conflict once they step onto the stage into the klieg lights; however, it is this very conflict which is needed to create the catharsis necessary for the healing of the consciousness of the world. Klieg lights have the ability to help create more *light* within us.

An excellent contemporary example is to be found in Colonel Margarethe Cammermeyer's willingness to stand up for herself as a lesbian, even though this meant being discharged from the U.S. Army. In June of 1994, the court found this action to be discriminatory and she was reinstated. While this finding will be appealed, new ground has been created on which all homosexuals now stand.

Yes, there was personal pain involved for her in the process of stepping on stage to play her part; however, the rewards of personal freedom for herself and for other homosexuals were far greater than the pain. It must also not be overlooked that the courage to produce her story by the producers of the television film, *Serving In Silence*, provided a potential for cathartic understanding and healing of the human consciousness through the compassionate and artistic treatment of this sensitive subject. Artists whom are supportive of such healing in the world are special blessings to the homosexual community and to the world at large for their work has the ability to speak to the heart and to inspire others.

It is the confrontation of prejudice coming from a space of love that heals. Fear-based attack can only create more of itself. It takes everyone, willing to play their part, to create more love in the world. Would anyone deny themselves to be a part of such a noble mission? They most certainly would not if they were only free enough from fear to begin the journey.

This is why it is so important for everyone to begin from where they are to heal their fears by releasing them through forgiveness. Once we move from 60 % fear to 40 %, we allow our capacity for love to increase from minority to majority. This will give us the strength to love and to trust others. This will enable us to step out on stage to play our role in life's drama, *Healing The Consciousness Of Humanity* by the Mother-Father Source, whatever that role is, in a manner which brings more love to the world.

As we do so, we continue changing more and more of our energy from fear to love and we help the world to heal. From the center of the soul, human beings truly wish to practice the Golden Rule. We can help everyone to do so by practicing it ourselves, as we become willing to play our supporting role in the Creator's drama in a supporting manner.

Your role is unique in all this world. It begins where you are now and evolves from your willingness to heal. This book and its ideas were written to help you in the healing process. It can also be helpful to your families, friends, employers, educators, ministers and legislators as they also heal their prejudices. As we become willing to heal and move to our next step, the Mother-Father Source will show us the way. All we need do is follow the path which creates more love in our lives and it automatically creates more love in the world.

As you begin releasing fear, you will be led to the particular thing which is next on your personal agenda. If you are a woman, perhaps your next step may be to become seriously involved in clear communication with those whom you believe to be in power in your life. To do so from a loving space can come only after a process of healing has taken place within yourself. If you have not canceled fear and restored yourself to love, it will be difficult to see others in that light.

If you are a homosexual of either gender, perhaps your next step in playing your unique role may be to "come out" to your parents, to special friends or to your employer. It may lead you to play a role in social issues, legislative change, education or spiritual endeavors. Whomever you are and wherever it leads you, this is your role in the drama for now. Playing it well will ensure that love continues to resolve fear in your life. Playing your part will certainly bring you many other roles to play. In so doing, you will find yourself living your *divine purpose*, flowing with the Creator's will and making this world a better place. Such action will inspire many others to join you in this process.

Women, who refuse to live their lives any differently than they ever have, can only expect more of the same treatment. Making their own productive changes, rather than trying to change others, will change their world for the better. Conquering fear is the only thing that stands in their way.

For homosexuals who are in the closet and who choose to remain closeted, living there will fail to offer the world an opportunity to heal and will fail them in healing themselves. The world needs you. It needs your honesty and openness to heal itself. It needs to know who you are and what you stand for and it needs to know that you are willing to treat others as you would be treated. It requires your fine example to eliminate its' prejudice. Nothing is accomplished by remaining silent or staying hidden for you need the world every bit as much as it needs you. So, start from where you are. Go as slowly or as quickly as feels right for you and continue the active involvement in the process of your own personal healing. Let this become the key for women to unlock their enduring silence about their needs in a patriarchal world through their own self love. For homosexuals, let this become the key that unlocks their closet to finally lead them out of "Egypt". Know that, as every prejudiced group finds their way to greater wholeness, thousands of others shall go with them. As everyone lifts themselves a little higher, others are also lifted. Together, this becomes change in the world.

The tendency has always been to try to change the world from the outside and this has never worked. The world changes when people change from the inside out. Fearful people can only create a fearful world. Loving people create a world which values love as, once more, like attracts like.

REFLECTIONS

Mother-Father Source of my being, I am committed to finding my Divine Purpose in life. Help me to learn to have holy relationships so that I overcome my personal fears with love. Help me to be a better communicator of love in the world. Mother-Father Source, help me to accept my mission of becoming light in the world by practicing the right treatment of others. Bless me with love and compassion especially when I am in the presence of those whom are not willing to express their light. Allow me to be a helpful factor in their healing and in my own.

*I shall speak to You each day. I shall listen to Your guidance and I shall act upon it. If You say "Go here, go there", I shall go. If You say "Do this, say that", I shall do so. I am willing to have You lead me to the light without resistance. Mother-Father Source, I am willing to begin my journey out of Egypt. I shall begin by releasing enough fear to be able to go forward so that I can play my role in Your drama. I shall make **Healing The Consciousness Of Humanity** the greatest play on earth.*

I know You are with me and that You will guide me from within so that I might learn more of love and its expression through the Golden Rule. This teaching is the standard by which I am prepared to live my life. I know that the more fear I release, the more able I am to become the expression of that beautiful standard in action.

Bless me and guide me in the development of Our relationship, Mother-Father Source. Develop my heart's capacity and commitment to right action in the world as I become a loving, human being who helps humankind to heal its prejudice through understanding and through love. Help me to see my errors and to release them through forgiveness. Let my life's example be an inspiration to all.

CHAPTER ELEVEN

Ending Prejudice

As we reinvent our Source devoid of prejudice and filled with *only* love and we use the Source as our role model, we cannot condone any form of prejudice in the world. We recognize prejudice as a barrier to love and it simply is not worthy of us. Irrational thoughts no longer rule us and there is nothing that would keep us from treating others as we would be treated. We recognize this as the truth of our being.

As ten of us embrace these ideas and act upon them, we allow ten more to create themselves through our example. Those ten then create ten more as love multiplies on earth. When enough love exists, the dams of prejudice shall break because they are not strong enough to serve as barriers to love. Perhaps it is no small coincidence that this is what we are now experiencing on the earth. Dams breaking and terrible floods may be only a metaphor for the deep healing of the human consciousness which is at hand. It is time for the old, unloving ways of prejudice to be finished. This will begin to be accomplished as the first ten of us step forward to create anew with our crayons made of love. Becoming again as little children and drawing inspiration from the Earth Mother and the Sky Father, we create a new picture of love by giving reverence equally to both.

Ten by ten by ten, the pyramid shall grow as we evolve in our understanding and love reigns on earth. As we begin right now to practice love, not fear; love, not hate, we hasten life's completion of love's understanding. For too long now, it has eluded us.

By 2012, the ancient Egyptian secrets of the pyramids are made known through life's experience and those of us who are here shall be capable of such understanding. It is the knowledge that like creates like. It always has. It always will and love can only create more of itself. This is the missing piece for which we have been searching. Putting this understanding into practice creates the time for which our souls have longed, the time when love, peace and harmony are life's experience, as we become consciously connected to each other and to the earth.

This is the time when we no longer create cancer running rampant through the rivers, oceans and the earth itself, which we try to justify and explain through cost effectiveness. It is the time of understanding cancer as the antithesis of love and as the fear it represents. As a human race, we refuse to continue dying from this fear or from the broken heart which it creates.

When love reigns on earth, our bodies and the very earth itself live healthfully together creating synergy and wholeness. Would we not choose to be a part of this new consciousness on earth? Would we not prefer to be an instrument of love instead of hate? Our wise inner self knows that this is the way home. We no longer choose to sing off key in life's great symphony. Only those without self love would seek to embrace irrational ideas and the prejudice they bring. Their only reason for doing so is to increase their own value but it is done in a way that is doomed to fail. It allows them to claim fool's gold as they live by the Pyrite Rule.

Everyone of us is on this ship in one way or another. We must get off because the iceberg cometh and because we can consciously decide to avoid participating in prejudice of any kind any longer. There is no valid reason for establishing barriers to love because we are One. Only when we refuse to allow these barriers to exist in our consciousness will we learn to love ourselves, and only when we love ourselves, will the barriers to love dissolve. This shall be our legacy to the next generation as we make a conscious choice for love and as we learn to be true to what we are. This is the only acceptable role model for our children.

We can easily see the beginning of prejudice as the first moment one member of the human race assigned a gender preference to the deity. This created the first false assumption from which many irrational thoughts were based. This established a false standard of "this is better than that". As long as we give life to this irrational thought by applying it to any segment of humanity through our beliefs and our actions, we contribute to more prejudice in the world.

Male is not better than female nor is the converse true. White is not better than black; the Aryan race is not better than the Jewish race; heterosexual is not better than homosexual. Disabled individuals are not of lesser value than mentally or physically perfect human beings, nor are the elderly less valuable than others. An "Animal Farm" mentality does not create anything but animals.

We have learned some of the lessons which a "better than" philosophy has produced by pondering some of the history of mankind. It has indeed been filled with intolerance and violence, justified by an equally prejudiced Creator, so mankind would have us believe. Those with a loving heart know that the Source of our being is not well served by such beliefs. They know the truth. In light of this, it was not the Jewish race who killed Jesus, but the spiritual pride and arrogance of a "better than" philosophy. Let us begin to see this for what it is, fear and judgment born of an irrational idea. It had no other choice but to culminate in prejudicial action. Let us begin to see this and all other less-than-loving actions for what they truly are: love longing for itself which failed to find completion because of barriers to love.

We can heal the past if we but learn to disallow every exclusion to love in the present. As every Christian embraces every Jew and every Jew embraces every Muslim and every Muslim embraces every Hindu and every Hindu embraces every Buddhist and every Buddhist embraces every Taoist and on and on and on..., love prepares to recognize and to create more of itself in the *New Millennium*.

Let us realize that, while there are many different forms of prejudice still gathering strength in an irrational world, there is one parent to them all. The irrational thought in the mind of humankind which first assigned gender to the Source of our being is the true parent of prejudice in the world. This formed a creative idea which was invalid. It was unworthy of the deity and it must now be corrected. It is the work which all of us are here to do.

As we correct our thinking that the Source does not truly give preference to any one gender, a major shift in our consciousness will occur. This consciousness shall give rise to many new ways of being in the world which shall expand and restore love on earth. All religions ascribing to only one gender in the Source will find themselves removing the Creator's limitations (and their own), or new ones shall be formed to initiate this process. When this correction completes itself, there will be an immediate shift in the increased expression of love on earth.

No longer will there be a fight over abortion for men will value the conscionable decisions women make regarding their own bodies as much as they value their own decisions. No longer will homosexuals live in their closet of fear because the elimination of the belief of prejudice in God banishes every other form of prejudice on earth. "Better than" has been replaced by "different from" and this dispels racial prejudice and other prejudicial forms as well. As irrational thought is lovingly replaced with truth, the family of humanity truly becomes a loving family once again. No longer are *traditional family values* embraced as an ethical model worthy of emulation, for they are recognized for what they have always been, values which have oppressed women, homosexuals, blacks and every other group which has not accommodated its "better than" philosophy.

It is possible that this change in consciousness could happen much faster if religions would take the lead in a speedy reformation of their beliefs and actions which are not loving and accepting of everyone. If they do not voluntarily do so, the iceberg will arrive to purge them of their ideas of prejudice in God. Spiritual pride and their attachment to being "right" may keep them from doing so but it does not have to be this way. Their decisions on this issue will become very easy to see, less by their rhetoric and moreso by their works. Established religions shall become either relevant or irrelevant in a loving world.

In the meantime, all prejudiced groups must come out and stand up for their right to be equally and lovingly esteemed. This coming out and standing up must not be done from anger and violence for these are the tactics of the opposition and they shall only bring more of what they are. Prejudiced groups and all individuals whom are committed to ending prejudice must respond out of love if this is what they would create.

This response must be profound and it must be ongoing. Women must continue to voice their opinion on their right to control the choices made about their bodies. They must see the argument used by religious men (and women they have convinced) as irrational. This self-righteous idea is based upon the idea that they know, without a shadow of a doubt, the exact moment when the soul enters the body. It is but another example of man attempting to be God. If one removes this facet of belief from the argument, it can no longer remain a valid argument unless God is male. As women, and the men whom would support them, begin to see this for what it is and speak out with a clear understanding of the irrational idea from which the abortion issue springs, it will be resolved in a manner which is respectful of women. It is, after-all, a lack of trust in their ability to make the right decision which is at issue. Women are not the children of men. They are every bit their equal and should be respected as such.

Everyone agrees that a baby is a human being when it is born and, as such, this connotes to us a body, mind and spirit and the moral laws which are necessary to protect it. To have other opinions on this subject is everyone's prerogative, but to legislate, legally or spiritually, based upon those opinions is not rational. Women are no longer the chattel property of men. To legislate a woman's choice through laws or violence is to denigrate her capability to make a conscionable decision on her own behalf.

Women, and men whom would support them, should not accept a system which does not offer balance to all. It is time for all of us to realize that patriarchal (or matriarchal) religions and societies do not offer balance to 50 % of the population. This is why, as we grow in our capacity to love, we must also grow in our disapproval of our current system of patriarchy in all its different forms. Women being born from the rib of man is but patriarchy's idea of a virgin birth which does not deserve serious consideration just because a man said: "This is so". It has only served to diminish the value of women and to treat them with inequality and disrespect.

The control of abortion in a matriarchal society would be no better. It might very well legislate control over where and how men release their sperm, as women create a new version of where life of the fetus begins. One can imagine the endless appeals which would eventually find their way into the U.S. Supreme Court of all female judges. Is this point sufficiently made? We must simply stop the abuse of either gender by envisioning a loving deity, equally inclusive of both of them. Can anyone believe that this is not what the Source of our being intended?

Such a deity would certainly support both genders in their ability to make conscionable decisions regarding their own bodies. Until this becomes a reality which remains uncontested, women must continue doing the things which evidence their support for gender fairness and equality. Some ideas for consideration are the following.

1. Women should continue to stand up and speak out
   for what is right. This can be done in a loving
   manner.

2. Women should consider terminating
   their membership in associations
   (religious, political and otherwise),
   and relationships which do not support their
   right to make conscionable choices regarding
   their own bodies.

3. Women should consider it important to know
   the position of every candidate for political
   office on this issue and from where
   his/her political contributions have come.

4. Women should consider casting their vote
   for a candidate clearly committed to gender
   equality and then make that individual
   accountable for their actions. More women
   should enter the political process as candidates.

5. Women must remain strong in their resolve
   to recognize that any reason advanced against
   a woman's right to choose is simply spirituality
   incorrect.

While gender prejudice is the oldest form of prejudice, homosexual prejudice is far more extreme and far more difficult to overcome for one major reason. Women are visible; everyone knows who they are. Centuries of all forms of abuse (even death), have caused homosexuals to become invisible among the general population. This will continue to be the most unhealed of all forms of prejudice until homosexuals "come out of the closet" and stand up for their equal right to make conscionable decisions about their bodies. Homosexuals have also been prone to irrational thought. They have made man's irrational beliefs about them more important than the Creator's. Being homosexual is, after-all, the way the Source of their being created them to be.

Many heterosexuals whom are prejudiced against homosexuals believe them to be incapable of making conscionable sexual decisions. While this is no more true of homosexuals than it is of heterosexuals, the silence of homosexuals about their identity is the very factor which perpetuates their prejudice. Until the general population knows homosexuals as the conscionable human beings which most of them are, they cannot dissolve and release their irrational ideas about them.

As painful and difficult as it is to take the risk on rejection, this is what homosexuals must do for their own sake if they would help themselves and the world to heal. To live in fear of being known for whom one is negates self-love and is not life affirming. Homosexuals must be willing to take the risk and know that whatever the consequences, they shall be better off and emotionally healthier for doing so. They are the only ones who can lead themselves out of "Egypt". Once they do so, they can then begin to follow the same before mentioned five steps given to women to ensure their right to equality (with a few appropriate changes in the verbiage). Until homosexuals come out, the five steps remain essentially irrelevant and there is little hope for progress to be made in ending homosexual prejudice. As long as homosexuals remain in the closet, they remain in agreement that there is something wrong with their lifestyle. Homosexuals must become willing to participate in their own healing and they must remain accountable for the progress made.

Every other oppressed and prejudiced group can follow the same five steps to find their way to wholeness and to help the world to end its prejudice about them by first coming out and standing up for who they are. A Jew must not be afraid to be known as Jewish. An African American must not forget his/her race while living in a white world. A physically deformed person should not feel the need to hide his/her deformity and all can use the same five step process to keep on keeping on until the world catches up to what is right and what is fair for all. Failure to continue with the five steps because some progress has been made will surely lead to a reversal of that progress. This is the precarious position of the present moment as it relates to the rights of women, homosexuals, blacks, the disabled and other prejudiced groups.

Without constant rejection of irrational ideas until the majority heals its irrational thinking and makes a commitment to live by the Golden Rule, we shall continue to see the resurgence of anti-Semitism and other forms of racial prejudice, the loss of rights for women, the overturning of gay and human rights legislation (and general reluctance to protect homosexuals from prejudice through the legal system), modification of the laws which protect the disabled and backward momentum for African Americans. The signs are clearly present right now for every prejudiced group. The vigilance of the *March on Prejudice* must continue and can only be successful if it is done non-violently, with all the love and compassion that it seeks to create for itself.

What about gay marriage? What a volatile issue this has become! The opposition to this issue clearly emanates from a "better than" rather than a "different from" philosophical foundation. Why else would some heterosexuals be opposed to it? We need only go back to Chapter 1 to revisit the fact that this opposition is based upon irrational thought.

A larger concern is that much healing needs to be done before this issue can be clearly seen and resolved without prejudice. How about gay men and lesbians "coming out of the closet" and allowing the heterosexual population to know them as the ethical and conscionable people that they are? Should this not happen first? What about legislation in 41 states making it unlawful to fire an individual from his/her job just because of their sexual orientation? It would seem that these are bottom rungs on the ladder and important steps to be taken before the issue of gay marriage can be resolved. It is clearly on the roof top of the prejudicial ladder.

Yes, it is discriminatory to disallow vows of commitment in the eyes of Source of our being and society which bring legal equality to the union in the same manner of heterosexual couples but one cannot get from A to B without traversing the distance in between. The world is not ready to deal with the flower of its prejudice without giving serious cultivation and healing to the roots from which it springs.

REFLECTIONS

Mother-Father Source of my being, help me to come out and stand up against prejudice in the world. There can be no acceptable excuse for not doing so which would be pleasing in Your eyes. Help my eyes to see the truth of this, to hold fast to it and to always act upon it in the world. Help me to voice my opinion from a loving perspective.

May I always clearly support every brother and sister still held captive in "Egypt". May I always do and say all that I can so that everyone knows that I stand for love and equality for all people. The evidence of my non-participation in a "better than" philosophy is crystal clear by the actions of my life.

Mother-Father Source of my being, I am willing to heal any last vestiges of irrational thoughts within myself. As I do so, I give courage to the world that it too can heal itself of every idea that ever stood as a barrier to love. Bless me now as I go forth to become a blessing in the world.

CHAPTER TWELVE

Your Message In The World

We create our message in the world by the thoughts we think. "As I think, so I do." Action is always precipitated by thought. Our actions show the world to us from our perspective. Our message in the world then becomes our thought materialized in form. When our thoughts are good (loving and non-injurious to others), our message speaks of goodness in the world; however, the message always begins with thought. Our thoughts create our world. It cannot be otherwise.

What is it that happens to us when we experience goodness? At some level, it stimulates our remembrance of the Source of all good. Sometimes this is a conscious remembrance. Sometimes it is not consciously remembered but it always reinforces, in some way, our connection with the Source of all good. The very words "Goddess" and "God" (aside from the cultural genderization of both words) actually come from the word "good". Goddess/God (The Source) is only good. There is no "sin" or error in the Source. "Sin" is purely man's invention.

If all of humankind were to truly emulate the Source, all of their actions would have to be good ones and their messages in the world would only speak of goodness because all of their thoughts would be good ones. Such activity would actualize the Golden Rule on earth. Treating everyone as we would like to be treated would easily emanate from the goodness within. If everyone were "here" in their consciousness, in the very heart of goodness, there could be no prejudice in the world. So, where in heaven's name are they?

The reality is that good does exist in the world and that each of us has experienced it at times. Some of us have experienced more of it than others. We have also experienced prejudice, either personally against us, as a bystander viewing its perpetration on others or as the perpetrators of prejudice ourselves. In fact, experiencing both goodness and prejudice at various times in our lives has helped us to fashion an ambiguous view of life and has helped to create conflict within us.

"How could the Creator (Goodness) allow such violence and atrocities to persist?" It is often a difficult pill to swallow when we realize that the Creator is not allowing these things to persist, we are! The Creator is only good. What then does this have to say about us? The point is that the Source is not responsible for this prejudicial mess on earth. We must accept responsibility for the monster we have created and we must change the world right now by changing ourselves. If our thoughts are not of goodness, we cannot create good.

Reflect for a moment on the goodness that you have experienced in your life and/or the goodness in the world of which you have become aware as one of us now begins to remember. I remember a time when I was a small child and I was very, very sick and my Mommy was there to put a cold cloth on my forehead, rub my feet, fix chicken soup for me (which I adore to this day) and sing me to sleep. I remember receiving my first bicycle. It was electric blue as it stood beside the Christmas tree, brighter than brilliant. How exciting it was to ride it for the very first time! How good it felt!

I remember the teacher who was so special in my eyes, the one who personified goodness to me, the one who took me aside and said just exactly the right thing at the right time to make me aware of the goodness in myself. I remember the time I was in the grocery store with my Dad and I was pushing the cart. Intending to make it through the check-out line as quickly as possible, I pushed my way in front of an elderly lady. My Dad gently pulled the cart backward, smiled at the lady and beaconed her to go in front of us. She smiled back and graciously accepted and this taught me more about goodness than anything I had previously experienced. To this day, I remember it as a great teaching regarding the treatment of others. It was an experience of goodness and it is one of the special things I shall always remember about my Dad. How gently he facilitated a teaching of goodness in me. As an adult, I remember reading about Mother Teresa and her dedication to helping others and it struck me as an example of goodness in the world.

These examples mentioned are but a few possible examples of one individual remembering personal experiences of good from life's experiences. You have your own memories (some of them may be similar) and your own examples of goodness which you have experienced. Reflect for a moment on five of the most important experiences of goodness which you have personally experienced before you read further. This reflection will make the ideas which follow more meaningful to you. It may seem like a pain in the neck to do while you are in the reading mode but the rewards are always greater when, rather than being told, you prove something to yourself. On a piece of paper, briefly describe your five most important experiences of goodness in a way that makes sense to you. It matters not that they may not make sense to anyone else. The examples already presented are used to illustrate this.

FIVE EXPERIENCES OF GOODNESS
1. Mommy when I was sick.
2. First bicycle.

3. Mrs. Morton in 6th grade.
4. Dad in grocery store.
5. Story of Mother Teresa.

Now, take a moment to write down your five examples. Have you finished? Are you sure? Good!

What do all of these items have in common? If you look at your examples of goodness (and mine), you will see that all of them were acts of giving. In doing so, they resonated the feeling of goodness in you as you subconsciously remembered (maybe also consciously) your connection with the Source of all good (the Mother Father Source who only loves and only gives). This remembrance strengthened goodness (love) in you.

It is important we remember that goodness is associated with giving and that giving is associated with the Source of all good. Rightly perceived, giving is a privilege and a responsibility which helps us to align more closely with the Source and with each other. Even when we receive, it is but an opportunity for someone else to give. Giving is what our message in the world is meant to be. Giving, for its own sake, is always associated with goodness and, as such, it is an integral part of our personal mission through our message in the world.

Look once again at your examples. Do any of your experiences of goodness extend prejudice against anyone or any group? There is a strong probability that they do not for goodness (love) and prejudice (fear) are two quite different energies. In fact, most of us can easily see the lack of goodness in prejudice and we can usually recognize and categorize it as such. It is granted that some of us have experienced more good in the world than others have but as long as we have had an opportunity to experience goodness at least once, it has had the opportunity to resonate goodness in us. This connected us with the larger body of good which is the Source and strengthened good in us. Because there is no prejudice in the Source, there can be no goodness found in prejudice.

Left to their own devices, all individuals have some innate sense of good because they are the child of a Mother-Father Source which is only good. This innate sense of good is what is sometimes referred to as our spark of divinity. It is what connects us to each other but we cannot see or feel this connection as strongly as possible as long as we consciously withhold love. The more prejudice we hold, the more separated we feel from others and from the Source. As long as we choose to hold prejudice, we cannot realize our Oneness with each other nor with our Creator.

Here is the really important part of all of this. We are all on a mission and it is essentially the same mission for each one of us. We have been sent out into the world by the Mother-Father Source of all good to re-discover the goodness in ourselves through our experience in the world. We have all the tools we need. We have had at least one experience in life which resonated the feeling of goodness in us so we know what it feels like and what we are trying to create. We also know that goodness feels good.

Our mission is then to go forth recapturing this feeling in as many different experiences as possible until we strengthen it so much within ourselves that we are able to live from this space. The mystics have called this the process of finding Oneness with God. It is actually finding Oneness with good. It is the pure and unadulterated rediscovery of the goodness in ourselves which has always been there. Here there is no room for prejudice for there are no irrational ideas to create fears, judgments and prejudiced actions in the world. There is only love. Arriving here, we can only treat others as we would be treated for we can only do what we are. We are one with the Source and every fiber of our being reflects this truth.

Having a frame of reference for goodness, we are on a mission to give that experience to everyone and everything we encounter, and not just through words, but through the way we treat each other. There is only one difficulty. Because we live in this messed up world, we have developed a frame of reference for prejudice. We have encountered it through others: our parents (they were not perfect), our human role models and through our religious and political institutions. These entities also learned it from others. As we saw in Chapter 1, prejudice is born from irrational thoughts, but to try telling that to someone who is in the process of having them is often like asking a welfare Mom to vote Republican. Prejudice is indeed a part of everyone's experience.

If we review our mission thus far of extending goodness in the world (the Golden Rule of treating others as we would be treated) for the purpose of realizing our Oneness with the Source and with each other, we encounter our establishment of a frame of reference for both goodness (love) and prejudice (fear). It is up to us to choose which master we shall serve. That to which we give more energy will grow stronger within us. This is how and where our free will becomes important. It often feels like war. We are foot soldiers on a mission of goodness, trying to make it through an area plied with land mines of prejudice and fear everywhere. The more afraid we become, the more we attack and this creates more war. The history of our civilization well documents the evolution of this journey.

Even though we can probably all agree thus far that humanity has failed to bring goodness to all that it has experienced, the mission is still the same. It is still out there for all of us to complete. It has not changed, nor can it. The mission is the mission. It is what all of us are here to do. We are to bring goodness (love) to all that we experience in the world so that we can resonate it and build our conscious memory of it in ourselves. "Oh yes, *this* is what I Am!" Our creative free will allows us to experience and to give out either love or fear. The more love we give, the more we become like the Source. The more fear we give (and we cannot give it unless we have it), the more barriers to love we erect in the form of our prejudices. Wouldn't you rather be Gandhi than Hitler?

Love brings us closer to the Mother-Father Source of our being and prejudice distances us from that loving Source. One of the most interesting of paradoxes is that many religions, sects within them, and religious and political organizations were formed and perpetuate themselves upon the foundations of prejudice. It is even more perplexing that sooner or later, most religious organizations attempt to become political. No wonder we are confused about goodness!

Patriarchal religions and religious groups have foundations in prejudice against women and against homosexuals. These are, without a doubt, the most prevalent, and the most extreme forms of prejudice in patriarchy, which unfortunately provide poetic license for many other prejudicial forms. All of them are antithetical to goodness. They are patriarchy's flight from love into fear and they provide examples of violence resulting from error. Prejudice against women and homosexuals are the "sins" (errors) of patriarchy, carefully constructed and projected into the world from the foundation of irrational thought. The good news is that humankind is not mandated to accept them. This is where free will becomes important. It provides a vehicle for choice. The choice for goodness can never be the choice for prejudice. These are but some of the land mines that we are to identity and avoid if we would successfully complete our mission.

Each choice that we make more clearly defines our message in the world. The substance and the purity of our message is entirely up to each one of us. We can get caught in the land mines, avoid them or defuse them. Whatever we do with them, we also do to ourselves, to our message in the world and ultimately, to the success of our mission. We came to bring goodness (love) to everything that we experience in the world. As we expand our abilities to discern the truth and act upon it, and not because someone in authority said that it is so, but because we know it to align with goodness (love), we shall find greater success with our mission and we shall become a positive role model for others. The world changes for the better as we change for the better. No longer should our lamentation only be for the violence of our children of today, but also for the good role models that we failed to provide for them.

In building our discernment of the truth as we use our free will to create and express goodness, there are some questions we might ask. A "yes" or "no" answer will be most helpful to us in arriving at the truth.

1. Does this idea, individual or this group totally align with goodness (love) or prejudice (fear)?

2. Does this idea, individual or this group exclude individuals or groups based upon fear?

3. Does this idea, individual or this group set limits on goodness (love)?

4. Does this idea, individual or this group invite me to be loving or fearful of anyone or any group?

5. Does this idea, individual or this group unite people or does it separate some from the rest?

6. Does this idea, individual or this group exclude anyone from power?

For some ideas, individuals and some groups, it is easy to answer with a simple "yes" or "no" and use our free will to easily align with them or avoid such alignment. For the vast majority of ideas, individuals and groups, it is often difficult (sometimes impossible) to arrive at a definitive "yes" or "no". Our answer more often is: "yes" about some things and "no" about others or a mixed bag. When this happens, the truth becomes aberrated and unacceptable. Unless we can say "yes", without reservation, to love or goodness, our association in silence with such ideas, individuals or groups is not a good idea. As an example, we shall explore some controversial subjects asking these questions.

1. **Subject of women as clergy in most patriarchal religions** - Does the exclusion of women as clergy align with goodness (love) or prejudice (fear)? **Answer:** *Well, it aligns with prejudice but there are some good reasons for it as noted by the church fathers, etc.*

2. **Subject of homosexuals in the classroom** - Is the avoidance of hiring homosexuals as teachers or firing them if they become known as such (even though they may be excellent teachers who have done no wrong)

based upon fear?   **Answer:** *Well, yes it is, but there are good reasons to fear them, etc.*

3. **Subject of a male Christian organization on the Christian message -** Does fighting initiatives on gay rights and excluding women from their organization set limits on goodness (love)? **Answer:** *Yes, maybe, but we do allow black males and we do empower all of them to go home and be all that they can be in the name of Jesus. Just because a leader of an organization takes a certain stand does not mean that we agree with him. Besides, there are good Biblical reasons for those ideas on gays and women.*

4. **Subject of Hitler (or anyone like him) on the Jews -** Does the idea that Jews are inferior and should be killed invite me to be loving or fearful of Jewish people? **Answer:** *Well, yes, maybe not loving, but there are good reasons for this, etc.*

5. **Subject of inter-racial marriage -** Does the idea that whites should not marry blacks unite people or does it separate some from others? **Answer:** *It unites whites and it separates blacks, but there are many good reasons why this should be done, etc.*

6. **Subject of abortion by Christian fundamentalists -** Does the idea that women do not have the right to make decisions about their own bodies exclude anyone from power? **Answer:** *Well, maybe, if you want to stretch a point, but what we are really talking about here is the baby's right, and, there are still many reasons why abortion is wrong, etc.*

We could go on and on with controversial examples on which a straight-forward answer of "yes" or "no" to our truth discernment questions seem impossible. "Yes, but..." or "No, but..." is but a facade for the masking of prejudice. It is also a rationalization for its presence. Knowing this is so, a loving heart must reject prejudice wherever it is found. These are the kind of questions we should be asking about all of the organizations and individuals with whom we associate. There simply is no acceptable reason for not treating all others as we would be treated. Unveiling this for what it is in truth is like unscrewing a nut on a bolt of fear. Unscrewing enough of them will allow the entire seat to be removed. It is a most important part of what our mission is all about.

Refusing to be a member of any group or ideology which does not meet our truth discernment standards for goodness is not an elective for our mission-completion course. It is required. Defusing these dangerous land mines of prejudice by taking a stand on these issues also helps others on their mission.

Our choices must be well contemplated and spiritually correct. Ideas, individuals or groups either advance goodness (love) in the world or they advance prejudice (fear). If we accept our mission as goodness (love), we must reject prejudice (fear) in all of its forms when and wherever we find it.

The world has lived too long with mutated standards. It is no longer acceptable to condone, rationalize or accept the part of the message that "sins" or falls short of the mark of goodness just because another part of the message is good. Oil does not mix with water. It is water that sustains us because it is primarily what we are.

Trying in vain to mix oil and water is the history of the ages. Thank heaven the Source is watching this "Rocky Horror" version of life and aware of the mess we have continued to create. Every now and then, out of pure goodness (love), the Source must say: "Their standards are becoming so mutated that they cannot see the truth. Looks like it might be time to send them another Master Teacher to show them by example what their mission is all about." Splat! "*Good grief*, they have just killed another one!"

We can plow through the horrifics of the past and find, in every instance, there was a mixed message with mutated standards in the driver's seat and, out of fear, we allowed it to exist. No one knows this better than women, homosexuals, blacks and Jews. Such conditions still exist but we can end the insanity of irrational thought right now "in the twinkling of an eye" by developing truth discernment standards and by acting upon them. The before stated questions may be of help as a template for truth recognition and identification but the bottom line of the "St. John Solution" is:

If it is not *ALL GOOD*; it's not good!

Relating this to the color spectrum, let us assume that goodness is blue and that prejudice is yellow. Mixing them together produces green. For the color to remain blue, we cannot add one speck of yellow. Even though the world has accepted green as the gold standard for centuries (pun intended), we can easily see what this has produced and we can recognize it as an aberration of the truth. There is no possible dilution.

If it is not *ALL GOOD*; it's not good!

Discerning the truth, standing for it and taking action upon it will end fear and prejudice in the world. Do you not desire to be a part of this great process or do you choose to continue doing business as usual while you try to dodge the land mines? Boom! There goes Oklahoma City! What will it take for all of us to WAKE UP? We must dissolve the irrational thoughts which give rise to bad ideas. More importantly, we must change our message in the world from fear to love.

We must see clearly and have the courage of our convictions to take action upon the ideas and groups which display incongruence. A good example of this is found in the action of Ex-President George Bush. After 30 years of membership in the National Rifle Association, he resigned his membership because of their prejudiced beliefs and actions regarding the U.S. government. This kind of principled action is what it will take to end all forms of prejudice on earth. It will take all of us, doing our work publicly so that we may become a *light* for others.

There are difficulties to be overcome in this process of change but every single one of them is personal. You will recall in the beginning of this chapter, it was mentioned that the substance of our message begins with thought. Whose thoughts do you think they are? "You mean I cannot cite parental abuse for killing my parents? You mean I cannot blame her death on her morality or on a racist policeman? You mean I cannot blame 17+ women for a Senator's sexual misconduct? Oh Lordy, where does that leave me?"

It leaves you with no defense and no excuse for whatever it is your thoughts have created in your world. You behold your creation as you examine your message. It is either a message of goodness (love) or prejudice (fear) and it has created itself as once more, like has attracted like and life has become exactly what you are.

Now is the time to examine your message accepting 100% responsibility for whatever it is. It never was, it never has been anyone else's fault. We cannot even imagine how the world would change if everyone acted as if this were true, for even 24 hours. It would lead us straight to the thoughts we hold as our beliefs. The beliefs which create fear in us stem from irrational thought(s). These give rise to the judgments we make about others and the prejudices we embrace. These thoughts are the things which give rise to our actions in the world. Our irrational thoughts are at cause and our prejudices are their effect. They continue to abort our mission over and over again. If we would but change the cause, the effect would change. Living in a violent world merely tells us that we have violent thoughts which have created violent actions.

Using the four step Prejudice model in Chapter 1 will help you to identify the truth about yourself. There is no better time than now to face it. It is time to stop dancing in the dark. Beginning at any step of the process will lead you to the other steps. Plug in the data as your mind presents it to you. This is but one difficulty to be overcome as you refine your personal message of goodness (love) in the world.

Another large area of difficulty is the area of prosperity and abundance, or the lack of it. It is difficult to focus on other issues when there is "not enough". While this also adheres to the fact that your thoughts create your world, there are other dimensions of this problem to contemplate. The lack of prosperity and abundance can lead you to become resentful of others more prosperous than you. This may encourage you to become prejudiced against prosperity, compounding the amount of irrational thoughts you already have on this subject. Such a vicious cycle maintains and increases a poverty consciousness in the world. Since the major wealth of the country is held by approximately 5% of the population, we can assume that, to varying degrees, this is more of a problem than it appears to be.

A poverty consciousness affects your message in an adverse manner. Changing your irrational thoughts about money, prosperity and abundance will help you to have more of them. If you feel that the lack of prosperity is a tremendous hurdle for you to overcome right now, consider availing yourself of the best prosperity teacher there is: Unity minister, Rev. Edwene Gaines. She and her husband, Bert Carson, have an excellent audio cassette series available called: *Prosperity Plus Bert*. You may learn of its availability through the reference section.

For all those who could use more prosperity and abundance in their lives, this cassette series is highly recommended. It should be of great help with the prosperity part of your mission. Treat yourself to the ideas which, if practiced, will end your lack of abundance. You deserve it!

What about forgiveness? "Whose?" Are you worried about the sawdust in someone else's eye when you have a two-by-four in your own? You are here to become a teacher of goodness (love) to all by your own example. This requires you to forgive yourself for every fearful thought, word and deed of your own creation and to responsibly own that, if it is in your own experience, you have created it. This is how you end the prejudice (fear) in you and this is how you return yourself to love. This is not a wam-bam process but rather a progression on a continuum of fear and love (prejudice and goodness).

In a progression toward any goal, there is something magical about passing the half-way mark. It's second wind time and it feels like you can run even faster than you have already. It also becomes easier to dodge bullets and land mines. Once you pass the 50 yard line, you are no longer starting the mission; you are on the way home!

Prejudice (fear)   50 Yard Line   Goodness (love)

*

*

*

Here is the way this works. When you have done enough forgiveness of self to release enough fear to make it beyond the 50 yard line toward goodness, it is easier to use discernment to see the truth of individuals, groups and ideas in general. Then, when you encounter a controversial subject, you will desire to ask a truth discerning question. If the answer is a "yes, but..." or a mixed bag of any kind, you will automatically see green. You are immediately able to recognize the mutation for what it is (cancer as opposed to healthy cells).

Once you make that recognition, you are unable to accept such ideas, and/or the individual(s) espousing them, to be goodness. You know the truth and you are able to see it clearly. Try as you may to forget it, you cannot stop the bottom line of "St. John Solution" from reverberating in your mind.

If it is not *All Good*, it's not good!

If it is not *ALL GOOD*, it's not good!

If it is not <u>*ALL GOOD*</u>, it's not good!

There is only one way to stop this reverberation and that is to do something about it. If you are a member of such a group, you may feel determined to resign your membership and compelled to state your reasons why. Publicly is best as it may help others to expand their understanding. If such a group is soliciting your membership, you may take delight in saying, "No Thanks!" If you are married to such a person, you may leave. No one deserves to live in fear. If you are a member of such a church, you may find another. By the way, could this be how the saying "right church, wrong pew" came about? If so, you are merely correcting it to be "wrong church, right pew". If you are a journalist, you may write about these ideas and you will be of immense help to others in seeing the truth of the matter. If you are a doctor who performs abortions, you may step gingerly around the defrocked-minister land mines of prejudice and continue on your mission. The timing on their mechanism is already set for self-destruct and there is nothing you can do about this. If you are a politician, boy, are you in trouble!

153

Politicians have one of the most difficult roads to travel on their mission to goodness. There are more land mines per square foot than there are fleas on a dog's back and these things can sometimes be inter-related. Every time a flea scratches their back, if they aren't careful, they can step on a land mine. They are vulnerable, extremely vulnerable if they have ever had sex with anyone, and holding the position of Speaker of the House seems to have very bad Karma attached to it.

All levity aside, it is probably more difficult for politicians than it is for any other group to stand on the truth discernment standards as put forth in this chapter. There are so many "green temptations" which seek them out on a daily basis. Everybody wants something from them and they are willing to place a value on their concerns. Politicians are human like the rest of us and this cannot always be an easy situation. It is far worse than a kid in the candy store. With politicians, the candy store follows them around. The honest politicians, and there are many, have the potential to quickly make great progress on their mission of goodness for they encounter twice as many land mines as the average person about which they make the right choices. This gives them many opportunities to refine and strengthen their message as they pursue their own mission of goodness in the world.

The truth of the matter is that there is no other group who has the potential to do more good. Politicians can be the real Trail Blazers on the path of goodness for themselves and for our nation by always allowing their legislative ideas to reflect truth discernment standards for everyone and by always having the courage to do the right thing. The end does not justify the means.

It also seems important to note that politicians are just like the rest of us. Before they are capable of doing "the right thing", they too must be beyond the 50 yard line toward goodness before they are able to recognize it as "the right thing". It is our responsibility to determine their progress in this regard before we elect them. Once elected, we should then support them with our prayers and our good will but we must also hold them accountable for their actions. While they represent us, they are morally responsible for the actions which they take. Legally, they are responsible for whatever the law requires.

In light of this, what happened before they became a candidate for public office should not be as morally important as what is happening now. People make mistakes and they often grow from them; however, a career politician with years of sexual abuse, while in office, should not be returned to public office again and again and should clearly not be shielded by his party because the offender happens to be politically useful. Taking part in this ignoble idea is like purposely stepping on a land mine.

The end can never justify the means in truth discernment standards because truth is not relative. While it may be more difficult to apply truth discernment standards in politics, there is no other area where more potential good for all humanity becomes possible. Politicians hold within their grasp the ability to end the many forms of prejudice and to heal the wounds of history. Failing to rise to this potential is the biggest land mine on their own mission home. May the Mother-Father Source strengthen their loving hearts and bring a clarity of vision enabling them to easily spot and remove the land mines of prejudice for all people. May politicians become catalysts for the Golden Rule by becoming *one* with it, personally and politically.

In light of this, we are at a precarious moment in the political history of this country. There are great dissatisfactions with both parties, especially on the issue of campaign reform. Without corrections, the time is ripe for a third party to capture the imagination of the people. In many ways, Ross Perot has served as the conscience of the nation speaking out on valid issues of great concern to all of us. Those whom would prejudice no one abhor the Republican alignment with the religious right. What is it that the Democrats really stand for? Both Republicans and Democrats must walk the talk on the issue of campaign contribution reform to regain the trust of the people. If parties are but a metaphor for the money and power of special interest groups, they are no longer relevant to the people.

The Democrats have exemplified *giving* (sometimes irresponsibly) while the Republicans have personified *receiving* (often greedily). All of life (even politics) is but a continuum striving for balance and the Democrats and Republicans are generally viewed at each end of the continuum. Both have lost touch with the people they represent. Without major reform, America is ripe for a third party to cull the weeds of both parties to combine the best of both energies.

A successful third party will be a good financial manager who cares about the people, who gives responsibly out of goodness and who believes in accountability. This party will have both a loving heart and a disciplined mind. It will symbolize commitment to the balance of the masculine and feminine principles of giving and receiving, both within itself and within its leaders. It will symbolize a balance in giving and receiving for all people and it will not align with prejudice of any kind. Human rights shall clearly be extended to all. It will not be known as the party of the rich or the party of the poor. A successful third party must truly be the party of *all* people.

Instead of an elephant or a donkey (which has thus far only symbolized an "Animal Farm" mentality), the symbol of this successful third party will be one of balanced scales, achieved through love for all humankind. This party of balance will inspire all people beyond the 50 yard line of goodness because it shall mystically resonate as the truth of their own being.

As it does so, a third party dream of victory can bring a clear and decisive victory in the next election if major reform is not enacted within the Democratic and Republican parties. Such ground cannot be gained on the back of any form of prejudice. There is simply too much goodness in the world to allow this to happen. There are too many people who are committed to discerning the truth, to acting upon it and to talking about it.

What might this third party look like? There could be a woman and/or a black, Jew or a homosexual on the ticket with no one emerging from the status quo of political life (as we know it), or from the military or religious organizations. **A loving heart and a clear stand against prejudice of any kind will be mandatory.** A personalized, mutated agenda cannot emerge as victorious in a world which values good. The party and the candidates cannot stand for the end of some prejudicial actions and not all of them. They cannot be for affirmative action and against human rights for gays and lesbians. They cannot be for ending racial discrimination and oppose a woman's right to make choices about her own body. Prejudice shall at last be clearly seen as prejudice and all of it shall be unacceptable.

If it is not *ALL GOOD*, it's not good!

A winning third party must be different from the status quo and must inspire the trust of all people. It must have a commitment to absolute integrity and to the implementation of responsible change which is devoid of prejudice against anyone.

The congressional seats up for grabs in such a scenario in 1998 will usher more women and people of all colors and sexual orientations. These shall be individuals who already wear a badge of scales upon their hearts and are committed to balance, as evidenced by their lives right now. With such persons involved in the political process, our country shall change for the better.

Without reform, the old Democratic and Republican parties will find themselves crumbling away and a one party system will begin emerging which becomes a clear and effective balance of giving and receiving.

Our currency will read: "In the Source of all Good, we trust". Our eyes can clearly see the truth. No longer are we dancing around the land mines. We are completing our mission of goodness in the world. We are on to something good and we are on the way home!

This kind of political party shall become victorious and replace what we now know as the politics of fear if our current political parties do not reform themselves. The off balance far ends of the continuum of giving and receiving are not, in any way, representative of balance. If, as a people, we are to identify with a goal of balance within ourselves, we shall certainly demand it of all those whom would represent us. The Democrats can not continue without a willingness to reconcile their checkbook any more than the Republicans can remain as a lobby for big business and the financially advantaged. Both parties must be willing to also embrace a mission of goodness (love) for our nation and that means leaving behind all forms of prejudice for all people.

In addition to our politics, we, as individuals, must heal all of our irrational thoughts and we must free up the dark energies, those expressions of the past that use to express through us. They have stood in the way of our ethical treatment of others and they are no longer acceptable. These dark energies never were our true nature and we can choose to consciously be what we really are: the expression of goodness in the world and a blessing to everyone. Once we have healed the major categories of irrational thought that exist within us about sex, power and money (what other real problems are there?), we can get on with our real mission in life. This mission is one of responsibility and service: responsibility to everyone for goodness and ethical treatment and service to the world through our own example. Can life become any sweeter than this?

Our primary responsibility is to accept all that we are as our own creation. No one else is to blame for anything in our lives. Here comes the kicker! We must become willing to change all of the things about ourselves which are not reflective of goodness (love). In doing so, we must release our prejudices about everyone and everything. "Such and such is not better than ...; it is simply different from ..." Our expanded awareness, at last, enables us to understand that the prejudices we hold say more negative things about *us* than they do about those whom we fear. This loving awareness prepares us to serve all of our fellow human beings, in every way possible, with all the love that we are.

REFLECTIONS

Mother-Father Source of my being, thank You for Your existence in my life as my Inner Teacher. Help me to strengthen Your presence through my willingness to change and grow. Your guidance always leads me to become more of what I am. Help me to always make the choice for goodness among the many temptations of the world because goodness (love) is my true nature. I am willing to always be a force for good in the world.

My message is my own expression of what I have allowed myself to become. If there is anything within my message which does not strive for the fair and ethical treatment of all others as I would myself be treated, let me see it clearly now and realize that this is not worthy of my energy. I am willing to free up that energy for my mission of goodness in the world. Help me to identify the land mines of prejudice and, in addition to avoiding them, help me to also diffuse them with Your love.

Peace, love and forgiveness precede, engulf and follow me as I now walk into all worlds of the past, present and future. They are my finest expression, my offering of myself to myself and to everyone I meet. As I do so, I help to shine Your Light upon life's path, too long darkened, as I complete my journey home.

YOUR SYMBOL OF COMMITMENT

If you align with the ideas in this book and you would like to display a visual symbol of your willingness to implement these ideas in your life, you may order an attractive lapel pin as a remembrance of this. Wearing it will remind you and speak to others of your commitment to the Golden Rule. It will also show that you are interested in doing your part to end all forms of prejudice on planet earth.

This pin is lapel size (actual size not shown) with a white background. The logo background is in purple with the hands and bird appearing in white. The square shape speaks of the four corners of the earth and the color purple is associated with healing, wisdom and spiritual truth. The hands indicate a balance of giving and receiving, a symbol for the actualization of the Golden Rule on earth. The bird indicates peace, both within the self and in the world as you joyously share your message of goodness (love) with others.

Pins are available for $13.95 each, five for $50.00 or ten for $90.00 which includes shipping and handling. They make an excellent gift for those you love. Each pin comes with a description of its meaning. To order, send your request with your check or money order, payable to the *St. John Institute.* Our address appears on the last page of this book.

This logo is a Registered Trademark of the St. John Institute.
Prior approval is necessary for other uses of this trademark.

Blessings!

APPENDIX I: REFERENCES

Armstrong, Karen, *A History of God*, (New York, Ballantine Books: 1993).

Ashlag, R. Yehuda, *An Entrance To The Tree Of Life*, Compiled and edited by Dr. Philip S. Berg, (Israel: Research Centre of Kabbalah: 1977).

Coptic Text Established and Translated by A. Guillaumont, H.-CH. Puech, G. Quispel, W. Till and Yassah 'Abd Al Masih, *The Gospel According To Thomas*, (New York, Harper and Row: 1959).

Editorial Staff of LIFE, *The World's Great Religions*, (New York, Golden Press: 1967).

Eisenman, Robert H. and Wise, Michael, *The Dead Sea Scrolls Uncovered*, (New York, Barnes & Noble Books: 1994).

*** Foundation for Inner Peace, *Course In Miracles*, (New York: 1975). May be ordered from the foundation at P.O. Box 635, Tiburon, CA 94920.

Fox, Emmet, *The Sermon On The Mount*, (New York, Harper Collins: 1989).

*** Gaines, Edwene and Carson, Bert, *Prosperity Plus Bert*, (Audio Cassettes by Produced by Prosperity Products, P.O. Box 294 Mentone, Al 35984).

Gomes, Peter J., *The Good Book*, (New York, William Morrow and Company, Inc.: 1996).

James, E. O., *The Cult Of The Mother-Goddess*, (New York, Barnes & Noble Books: 1994).

King James Version, *The Holy Bible*, (Nashville, Tenn., The Southwestern Company: 1966).

Kyokai, Bukkyo Dendo, *The Teaching of Buddha*, (Tokyo, Japan, Bukkyo Dendo Kyokai: 1966).

Jampolsky, Gerald, *Love Is Letting Go Of Fear*, (Milbrae, California, Celestial Arts: 1979).

Millay, Edna St Vincent, *Collected Poems*, (New York, Harper and Brothers: 1956).

Life Application Bible, King James Version, (Wheaton, Illinois, Tyndale House Publishers, Inc.: 1989).

Morris, William, Editor, *The American Heritage Dictionary Of The English Language*, (Boston, Mass., Houghton Mifflin Company: 1976).

Nicoll, Maurice, *The New Man*, (Baltimore, Md., Peguin Books, Inc: 1967).

*** Ryce, Michael, *"Why Is This Happening To Me... Again?!"*, a four hour workshop available on audio and video cassette. *Book by the same name is also available. For a current and complete listing of the availability of his work, write to: Dr. Michael Ryce, Rt. 3, Box 247, Theodosia, MO 65761. (417) 273-4838 R 1987.*

Schoeps, Hans-Joachim, Translated from German by Richard and Clara Winston, *The Religions of Mankind*, (U.S.A., Doubleday Anchor: 1966).

Stone, Merlin, *When God Was A Woman*, (New York, Barnes & Noble Books: 1993).

Smith, Huston, *The Religions Of Man,* (New York, A Mentor Book: 1961).

St. John of The Cross, *Dark Night Of The Soul*, Translated and edited, with an introduction by E. Allison Peers, (U.S.A., Image Books: 1959).

The Word In Life Study Bible, New Testament Edition, (Nashville, Tenn., Thomas Nelson Publishers: 1993).

Thomma, Steven and Cannon, Angie, *"A Nation Awash In Worry"*, St. Petersburg Times, (St. Petersburg, Florida, Times Publishing Company: October 30, 1994).

Waley, Arthur (Translation), *The Analects of Confucius*, (London, Allen & Unwin, 2nd ed.: 1945).

Watts, Alan W., *The Way Of Zen*, (New York, Vintage Books: 1957).

Yogananda, Paramahansa, *The Science of Religion*, (Los Angeles, Self Realization Fellowship: 1974).

*** *Recommended courses of study for those individuals who align with the ideas presented in this book.*

APPENDIX II.

Services and Other Products Offered By:

The
St. John

Institute ®

Educational Services

Dr. Sandra St. John is available for lectures, workshops and speaking engagements. If you or your organization are interested in scheduling these services, you may write to her or communicate through Email at:

stjohn33@aol.com

To be placed on our mailing list and notified of any "St. John Happenings" in your area, please send us your name, address and telephone number with your request through Email or the U.S. Postal Service. Our mailing address appears on the last page of this book.

The Gift of
BARRIERS TO LOVE

contains:

The book, **BARRIERS TO LOVE**

and a

SYMBOL OF COMMITMENT Lapel Pin

*Attractively Packaged To Make An Excellent Gift
For Someone You Love*

$27.95

Includes Postage and Handling
First Class Mail

Send your request with check or money order payable to:
St. John Institute

Our address appears
on the last page of this book

THE HOMOPHOBIA HEALING KIT

Affirming Insights
From A Spiritual Perspective
by
Dr. Sandra St. John

Contains the book:
THE HOMOPHOBIC HEALER
A Primer for Gays, Lesbians, the Families and Friends
Who Love Them

plus

Affirmations For Personal Healing

This set of 42 affirmation cards comes with instructions for their use. Each card is the size of a business card. The affirmation cards may be used by themselves or in conjunction with other tools for spiritual development. *Affirmations For Personal Healing* offers an expansive experience in personal growth.

Attractively Packaged To Make An Excellent Gift
For Someone You Love

———————————

$19.95

Includes Postage and Handling
First Class Mail

———————————

Send your request with check or money order payable to:
St. John Institute

YOU MAY ORDER INDIVIDUAL ITEMS
Items Sent First Class Mail

____

Specify Number of Items

BOOKS:

______   **THE HOMOPHOBIC HEALER** ----------------------$ 8.95

______   **BARRIERS TO LOVE** ----------------------------------$13.95

AFFIRMATION CARDS:

______   **Affirmations For Personal Healing** ---------------------$ 8.95

LAPEL PIN:

______   **Symbol of Commitment Pin** -----------------------------$ 9.95

Number of Items ---------- ________

Postage and Handling ------ ________
Add $4.00 up to a $14.00 order.
Add $1.00 for each additional
$7.00 worth of products.

TOTAL ENCLOSED ------ ________

Enclose Check or Money Order payable to the St. John Institute.
Mail to us at:

St. John Institute
P.O. Box 189
Murrayville, GA 30564

____

St. John Institute Email Address: **stjohn33@aol.com**